Annotated Teacher's Edition

# WORLD OF VOCABULARY

BLUE

Sidney J. Rauch

Alfred B. Weinstein

Assisted by Muriel Harris

## Photo Credits

## World of Vocabulary, Blue Level, Third Edition

**Sidney J. Rauch** • **Alfred B. Weinstein**

Copyright © 1996 by Globe Fearon Educational Publisher, a division of Paramount Publishing, One Lake Street, Upper Saddle River, New Jersey 07458. All rights reserved. No part of this book may be reproduced or transmitted in any form or by any means, electrical or mechanical, including photocopying, recording, or by any information storage and retrieval system without permission in writing from the publisher.

Printed in the United States of America

2 3 4 5 6 7 8 9 10      99 98

ISBN: 0-8359-1303-1

# CONTENTS

## >>>> Program Overview

The eight levels in the *World of Vocabulary* series are especially designed to interest ESL/LEP students and students who have been reluctant or slow to expand their vocabularies. As an effective alternative to traditional vocabulary development programs, each lesson in *World of Vocabulary* offers:

- a short, high-interest, nonfiction article that incorporates the key words for that lesson in a meaningful context.
- photographs that hold students' attention and provide additional context for the key words.
- a variety of short skills exercises that build understanding and retention.
- high-interest writing and simple research projects that offer opportunities for students to extend their learning.

This revised edition of *World of Vocabulary* includes new and updated lessons at all levels and a *Diagnostic and Placement Guide* to aid diagnosis and placement within the *World of Vocabulary* series. New stories in all eight levels spotlight personalities, such as Jim Carrey, Sandra Cisneros, and Steven Spielberg, and cover topics as engaging as World Cup soccer, Navajo code talkers, "Star Trek," and a group of Los Angeles teenagers who make and sell "Food from the 'Hood."

The revised series continues to offer diverse subjects and now includes selections on Latino actor Edward James Olmos, African American writer Walter Dean Myers, Native American ballerina Maria Tallchief, Latino baseball legend Roberto Clemente, Puerto Rican writer Nicholasa Mohr, and Chinese American writer Laurence Yep.

All eight levels continue to have color designations rather than numbers to prevent students from identifying the books with grade levels. The use of color levels also enables teachers to provide individual students with the appropriate reading skills and vocabulary enhancement without calling attention to their reading levels. Below are the revised *World of Vocabulary* levels listed by color and reading level:

| | |
|---|---|
| Yellow | 3 |
| Tan | 4 |
| Aqua | 5 |
| Orange | 6 |
| Blue | 7 |
| Red | 8 |
| Purple | 9 |
| Green | 10 |

As in the earlier version of *World of Vocabulary*, some lesson elements are carried throughout the series, but the pedagogy and design of each book is geared to the needs of students at that level. For example, the Yellow and Tan books are set in a larger typeface and have more write-on space for student responses than the other six books. Each lesson in these first two books contains eight key vocabulary words, compared to ten key words in the other books.

The Yellow and Tan books also include 15 units rather than the 20 units in the other books in the series. "Using Your Language" exercises in the Yellow and Tan books teach fundamental language skills that may need reinforcement at this reading level. The Tan book adds a phonics exercise.

As the reading level progresses in the next six books, the exercises offer more vocabulary words and increasing challenges. For example, "Find the Analogies" exercises appear in some lessons at the Aqua, Orange, and Red levels but are a part of every lesson in the Blue, Purple, and Green books.

## >>>> The Need for Vocabulary Development

Learning depends on the comprehension and use of words. Students who learn new words and add them to their working vocabularies increase their chances for success in all subject areas.

Understanding new words is especially crucial for remedial and second-language learners. Their reluctance or inability to read makes it even more difficult for them to tackle unfamiliar words. The *World of Vocabulary* series was created for these students. The reading level of each selection is carefully controlled so students will not be burdened with an overload of new words.

Most importantly, the *World of Vocabulary* series motivates students by inviting them to relate their own experiences and ideas to the selections. In doing so, students gain essential practice in the interrelated skills of listening, speaking, reading, and writing. This practice and reinforcement enhances their vocabulary and language development.

## >>>> Key Strategies Used in the Series

### Providing Varied Experiences

The more varied experiences students have, the more meaning they can obtain from the printed word. For example, students who have studied the development of the space program will also have learned many new words, such as *astronaut* and *module*. They have also attached new meanings to old words, such as *shuttle* and *feedback*.

The reading selections in the *World of Vocabulary* series enable students to enrich their vocabulary by exploring major news events, as well as the lives and motivations of fascinating people. Through the wide range of selections, students encounter new words and learn different meanings of old words.

Visual tools are also valuable sources of experience. The full-page and smaller photographs in the lessons capture students' attention and help them to understand the words in the reading selections.

### Building Motivation

If we can create the desire to read, we are on our way to successful teaching. Formal research and classroom experience have shown that the great majority of students are motivated to read if the following ingredients are present: opportunities for success, high-interest materials, appropriate reading levels, the chance to work at their own rate, and opportunities to share their experiences.

All of these ingredients are incorporated into the *World of Vocabulary* lessons through the use of engaging reading selections, controlled reading levels, a range of skills exercises, and discussion and enrichment opportunities.

### Making Learning Meaningful

We do not often learn new words after one exposure, so vocabulary development requires repetition in meaningful situations. The *World of Vocabulary* series provides opportunities for students to use new words in relevant speaking and writing activities based on the high-interest reading selections.

### Fostering Success

When students feel they have accomplished something, they want to continue. The *World of Vocabulary* series is designed to help students gain a feeling of accomplishment through listening, speaking, reading, and writing activities that motivate them to go beyond the lessons.

## >>>> Readability Levels

The reading level in each lesson is controlled in two ways. First, vocabulary words appropriate to the designated reading level were selected from the EDL Core Vocabulary Cumulative List. The words were chosen for their interest, motivational level, and relevance to each reading selection.

Next, the reading level of each selection was adjusted using the Flesch-Kincaid Readability Index. This formula takes into account average sentence length, number of words per sentence, and number of syllables per word.

The new *Diagnostic and Placement Guide* provides an opportunity to diagnose students and place them into the appropriate levels of the series. The *Diagnostic and Placement Guide* offers tests that gauge students' vocabulary abilities and a scoring rubric to facilitate student placement.

# VOCABULARY STRATEGIES

## >>>> Learning and Thinking Styles

People of all ages learn and think in different ways. For example, most of us receive information through our five senses, but each of us tends to prefer learning through one sense, such as our visual or auditory modality.

By keeping in mind the different ways students learn and think, we can appeal to the range of learning and thinking styles. By taking different styles into account in planning lessons, we can help all students understand new information and ideas and apply this knowledge and insight to their lives.

There are three main learning styles:
- Visual learners like to see ideas.
- Auditory learners prefer to hear information.
- Kinesthetic or tactile learners absorb concepts better when they can move about and use their hands to feel and manipulate objects.

After we receive information, we tend to process or think about the information in one of two ways:
- Global thinkers prefer to see the "big picture," the whole idea or the general pattern, before they think about the details. They search for relationships among ideas and like to make generalizations. They are especially interested in material that relates to their own lives. Global thinkers tend to be

impulsive and quick to respond to teachers' questions.
- Analytical thinkers focus first on the parts and then put them together to form a whole. They think in a step-by-step approach and look at information in a more impersonal way. They are more likely to analyze information and ideas rather than apply it to their own lives. Analytical thinkers tend to be reflective and thoughtful in their answers.

However, few of us are *only* auditory learners or *only* analytical thinkers. Most people use a combination of learning and thinking styles but prefer one modality or style over the others. An effective lesson takes into account all three types of learning and both types of thinking. The ideas below, in addition to your own creativity, will help you meet the needs and preferences of every student in your class.

### Visual Learners
- Write the lesson's key vocabulary words on the chalkboard, overhead transparency, or poster so students can see the words and refer to them.
- Encourage students to examine the photographs in the lesson and to explain what the pictures tell them about the key words.
- Repeat oral instructions or write them on the board. After giving instructions, put examples on the board.

- Involve students in creating word cluster maps (see p. xiv) to help them analyze word meanings.
- Use the other graphic organizers on pp. xiii–xvii to help students put analogies and other ideas into a visual form.
- Display some of the writing assignments students complete for the "Learn More About..." sections. Encourage students to read each other's work.
- For selections that focus on authors or artists, collect books, pictures, or other works by that author or artist for students to examine.
- For selections that focus on actors, show videotapes of their movies or television shows.

### Auditory Learners

- Invite a volunteer to read aloud the selection at the beginning of each unit as students follow along in their books. You might audiotape the selection so students can listen to it again on their own.
- Ask a student to read aloud the "Understanding the Story" questions.
- Provide time for class and small-group discussions.
- Read aloud the directions printed in the books.
- Occasionally do an activity orally as a class, such as "Complete the Story."
- Allow students to make oral presentations or to audiotape assignments from the "Learn More About..." sections.

### Kinesthetic or Tactile Learners

- Encourage students to take notes so the movements of their hands can help them learn new information.
- Encourage students to draw pictures to illustrate new words.
- In small groups, have students act out new words as they say the words aloud.
- Invite students to clap out the syllable patterns and/or spellings of new words.

- Write (or have students write) the new words on cards that can be handled and distributed.
- Provide sets of letters that students can arrange to spell the key words.

### Global Thinkers

- Explain the "big picture," or the general idea, first.
- Point out how the key words fit patterns students have studied and how they relate to words and concepts that are already familiar to students.
- Involve students in brainstorming and discussion groups. Encourage students to express ideas and images that they associate with the new words.
- Explore ways that ideas and information are relevant to students.
- Encourage students to think about their answers before they respond.
- Set goals and offer reinforcement for meeting those goals.

### Analytical Thinkers

- Start with the facts and then offer an overview of the topic.
- Give students time to think about their answers before they respond.
- Encourage students to set their own goals and to provide their own reinforcement for meeting them.
- Suggest that students classify new words into several different categories.
- Provide time for students to organize concepts or processes in a step-by-step approach.
- Help students recognize how new concepts relate to their own lives.

## >>>> Cooperative Learning

One way to address multiple learning and thinking styles and to engage students more actively in their own learning is through cooperative learning activities.

Cooperative learning means more than having students work in groups. They must work together toward a shared goal that depends on each person's contribution. In cooperative learning, group members share ideas and materials, divide task responsibilities among themselves, rely on each other to complete these responsibilities, and are rewarded as a group for successful completion of a task.

If your students are not accustomed to group work, you might assign (or have students choose) group roles, such as discussion leader, recorder, reporter, or timekeeper. Having specific responsibilities will help group members work together.

Cooperative learning has many applications in the *World of Vocabulary* series. For instance, you might organize the class into groups and have each group teach its own members the key vocabulary words in that lesson. Groups could use a jigsaw approach, with each person learning and then teaching two or three words to other members of the group. Groups might create their own word searches, flashcards, crossword puzzles, incomplete sentences, analogies, and so on.

Then evaluate each group member to determine his or her level of understanding. Or you might ask group members to number off so you can evaluate only the 3s, for example. Explain that you will hold the entire group accountable for those students' mastery of the lesson words.

In other applications of cooperative learning, students might work together to create one product, such as a cluster map, a simple research project, or an original story that incorporates the key vocabulary words.

You might also consider trying the cooperative learning activities below, modifying them so they will be appropriate for your students.

**Word Round-Robin**

Organize the class into groups of ten (eight for Yellow and Tan levels) and have each group sit in a circle. Ask members to count off 1-10 (or 1-8) and give everyone a sheet of paper. Assign all the 1s one vocabulary word from the lesson, the 2s another word, and so on. Then follow these steps:

**Step 1:** Ask students to write their assigned word and their best guess as to its definition.

**Step 2:** Have students pass their papers to the person on their right. Then tell them to read through the story to find the word on the paper they received. Have students write another definition below the first definition on the paper, using context clues from the story.

**Step 3:** Ask students to pass their papers to their right. This time tell students to use a dictionary to look up the word on the paper they received. Then have them write on the paper the dictionary definition and a sentence that includes the word, using the same meaning as in the story.

**Step 4:** Invite groups to read each paper aloud, discuss the word, and write one definition in their own words, based on what members wrote on the papers.

**Step 5:** Have each group share its definition for the assigned word with the class. Discuss similarities and differences among the definitions. Guide students to recognize that definitions of some new words are clear even in isolation because of their root words, while others have multiple definitions that depend on the context in which they are used.

**Synonym Seekers**

Involve the class in preparing for this activity by assigning a vocabulary word to each pair of students. (You might include words from more than one selection.) Each pair will write its word and as many synonyms as possible on an index card, consulting a dictionary and thesaurus, if you wish.

Have pairs share their cards with the class, explaining subtle differences among the synonyms. Then collect the cards and combine pairs of students to form teams of four or six. Call out one of the vocabulary words and ask teams to write down as many synonyms as they can think of in 30 seconds.

Then read the synonyms listed on the card. Teams will give themselves one point for each synonym they recalled. Encourage students to suggest new synonyms to add to the cards and discuss why certain words could not be used as synonyms. Play the game several times with these cards before creating new cards with other words.

## >>>> Approaches for ESL/LEP Students

- Invite volunteers to read the stories aloud while students follow along in their books.
- Watch for figurative expressions in the lessons and discuss their literal and intended meanings. Examples include "making faces," "friendly fire," and "bounce off the walls."
- Help students identify root words. Involve them in listing other words with the same roots and in exploring their meanings.
- Compare how prefixes and suffixes in the vocabulary words are similar to those in words students already know.
- Make word webs to help students understand relationships among words and concepts. Use the graphic organizer on page xiv or write a vocabulary word in the center of the chalkboard or poster. Invite students to name as many related words as possible for you to write around the key word. Discuss how each word is related.
- Involve students in listing words that are similar in some way to a vocabulary word, such as other vehicles, adverbs, occupations, and so on.
- Encourage students to share words or phrases from their native languages that mean the same as the vocabulary words. Invite them to teach these words from their native languages to the class.
- Arrange cooperative learning and other activities so ESL/LEP students are grouped with students who speak fluent English.
- Periodically group ESL/LEP students together so that they can assist one another in their native languages.
- Foster discussion with questions, such as "Do you think our space program should send more astronauts to the moon? Why?" and "Would you like to perform in a circus? Why?" These kinds of questions encourage students to use English to share their ideas and opinions.

## >>>> Cross-Curricular Connections

### General
- Challenge students to identify vocabulary words that have different meanings in other subject areas. For example, *fins* are defined as "rubber flippers" in the Aqua book. How are *fins* defined in science?
- Give extra credit to students who find the lesson's vocabulary words in other textbooks or in newspapers and magazines. Discuss whether the meaning is the same in both uses.

### Math
- Invite pairs of students to write problems that include vocabulary words. The difficulty level will depend on their math skills. Ask pairs to exchange problems and try to solve each others'.

### Language Arts
- Encourage students to write letters to some of the people described in the stories. Ask them to incorporate some of the lesson's key words into their letters.
- Have students, working in pairs or individually, write their own stories, using a certain number of vocabulary words from one or more selections.

They might leave the spaces blank and challenge other students to complete the stories correctly.

- Organize a spelling contest, using vocabulary words.
- Have groups prepare crossword puzzles that will be combined into a book.
- Encourage students to conduct surveys and/or interview people regarding topics that stem from the stories. For example, how many students or staff at school collect trading cards? What kinds do they collect? How many students or staff are "Star Trek" fans? What attracts them to "Star Trek"? Encourage students to graph their findings and to write short reports explaining their conclusions.

# A SAMPLE LESSON PLAN

The following is a suggested plan for teaching a lesson from the *World of Vocabulary* series. You might use it as a guide for preparing and organizing your lessons. However, be sure to modify it where necessary to take into account your students' needs, abilities, interests, and learning styles, along with the specific exercises included in that lesson.

## >>>> Setting Objectives

Each lesson in the *World of Vocabulary* series is based on the objectives below.
- To create enthusiasm for and an understanding of the importance of learning new words
- To improve reading comprehension by teaching the meanings of new words, stressing context clues
- To improve vocabulary by presenting key words in exercises that range from simple to complex and that allow for reinforcement of learning
- To encourage oral expression and motivate further study by introducing a highly interesting topic.

## >>>> Stimulating Interest

Invite students to examine the photograph on the first page of the lesson. To stimulate their curiosity and involve them in the topic, ask questions. For example, if the lesson were about Koko the gorilla, you might ask:
- The gorilla in the picture is named Koko. How do you think Koko might be different from other gorillas?
- Do you think it is possible to teach a gorilla to talk? Why or why not?
- If Koko could talk to people, what do you think she might say?

## >>>> Reading the Story

Have students read the story, silently or in small groups. You also might assign the story to be read outside class. To help auditory learners and ESL/LEP students, ask a volunteer to read the story aloud while classmates follow along in their books.

Encourage students to use the context clues in the story and the opening photograph to figure out the meanings of several boldfaced words. You might have students suggest a definition for each key word, based on context clues. Write the definitions on the chalkboard so the class can review and modify them later in the lesson.

As an aid to ESL/LEP students, discuss words or phrases in the story that have more than one meaning or that have figurative meanings. Two examples in the story about Koko are "blew kisses" and "spends some time."

## >>>> Completing the Exercises

The information about exercises below is based on the lesson about Koko in the Orange level. However, books at different levels include different exercises. For example, the Yellow and Tan books offer a simpler activity called "Make a List" instead of the "Understanding the Story" exercise.

Students using the Yellow and Tan books also complete an exercise called "Find the Synonyms," while students at the Aqua, Orange, and Red levels have the "Complete the Sentences" exercise. The equivalent exercise for students at the Blue, Purple, and Green levels is called "Find the Analogies." Each level also includes a variety of other grammar and skills exercises.

Despite variations in exercises from level to level, the explanations below will help you understand why certain exercises are included and how they can be modified to support different learning and thinking styles.

## >>>> "Understanding the Story"

This exercise usually asks students to determine the main idea of the selection and to make an inference as a way of assessing their general understanding of the story. Remember that global thinkers may have an easier time describing the main idea than analytical thinkers, who tend to focus on the parts of the story rather than the whole idea.

To use this as a cooperative activity, have students discuss the questions in groups of two or three. Then pair two groups so they can share their conclusions. Ask groups that disagreed on the answers to tell the class the reasoning for their different choices. Be sure to clear up any misunderstandings that become apparent without squelching creativity.

To make sure all students understand the general content of the story, ask a volunteer to summarize it in a sentence or two. Then give the analytical thinkers in the class an opportunity to contribute by describing some of the key supporting details in the story.

## >>>> "Make an Alphabetical List"

This activity encourages students to study the key words closely and to become more familiar with their spellings. Practicing writing the words in alphabetical order will be especially beneficial for kinesthetic learners.

To check students' accuracy in arranging the words in alphabetical order, ask one or two students to read their lists aloud. Visual learners will appreciate seeing the list written on the board.

If necessary, model the pronunciation of certain words. Practice saying the more difficult words as a class. (This technique will also be helpful for ESL/LEP students.)

## >>>> "What Do the Words Mean?"

In this exercise, students match the definitions listed in their books to the lesson's vocabulary words. If students offer other definitions for the same words, encourage them to consult a dictionary to check their accuracy. Many of the key words have different meanings in other contexts.

Encourage students to suggest synonyms for the words and perhaps some antonyms. Analytical learners might enjoy identifying root words and listing other words with the same roots, prefixes, or suffixes. Many ESL/LEP students will also benefit from this analysis.

## >>>> "Complete the Sentences"

This exercise gives students another opportunity to practice using context clues as they complete a set of sentences using the key words.

### >>>> "Use Your Own Words"

Working individually or in groups, students are encouraged to brainstorm words that describe a picture or express their reactions to it. This exercise fosters creativity involves students in the lesson by asking for their personal responses. Their responses will depend on their prior knowledge and individual perceptions, so answers are not included in the Answer Key. You might use some of the graphic organizers on pages xiii–xvii for this activity.

As a cooperative activity, students might enjoy working with three classmates to write a group description of the picture. Tell the first group member to write a word related to the picture on a sheet of paper and to pass the paper to the right. Have the next two group members add their own words, different from the ones already listed. Then ask the fourth group member to write one sentence about the picture that includes all three words. Start another sheet of paper with a different group member and continue in the same way, with the fourth member combining the words into one sentence.

### >>>> "Make New Words from Old"

This is one of several reinforcement exercises throughout the *World of Vocabulary* series. "Make New Words from Old" invites students to look creatively at the letters in a key word from the lesson. Other exercises in the series challenge students to identify synonyms and/or antonyms, underline specific parts of speech, to find the subjects and predicates in sentences, to write the possessive forms of words, or to complete other activities that focus on key words from the lesson.

### >>>> "Complete the Story"

Students again use context clues to place the lesson's key words correctly in a new story. This story relates to the one that opened the lesson and may offer more information on the topic or encourage students to apply new knowledge or insights in their own lives. You might use "Complete the Story" as a post-test of student mastery of the key words.

### >>>> "Learn More About..."

The last page of each lesson offers one to four activities that encourage students to learn more about the lesson's topic. You might assign one or several activities or encourage students to choose an activity to complete for extra credit. They could work during class time or outside of class—individually, with partners, or in small groups.

Some of the activities are developed for ESL/LEP students, while others provide opportunities for cooperative learning, cross-curricular projects, and enrichment. Placing activities in these categories was not meant to limit their use, as many of the activities would benefit and interest most students. For some reluctant readers, these projects may be their first attempt at independent research, fueled by their interest in the lesson's topic.

Some lessons include a "Further Reading" activity that lists fiction or nonfiction books on the lesson's topic that are appropriate for that reading level. Students are asked to complete a brief activity after their reading.

"Further Reading" and other activities that require a written response provide additional opportunities for students to practice and receive feedback on their writing skills, including punctuation, capitalization, and spelling. The effort students spend on the "Learn More About" activities can result in marked improvements in their reading and writing skills.

>>>> The topic of the story:

>>>> The main idea of the story:

>>>> Some details from the story:

>>>> What interested me most:

>>>> A question I would like to ask:

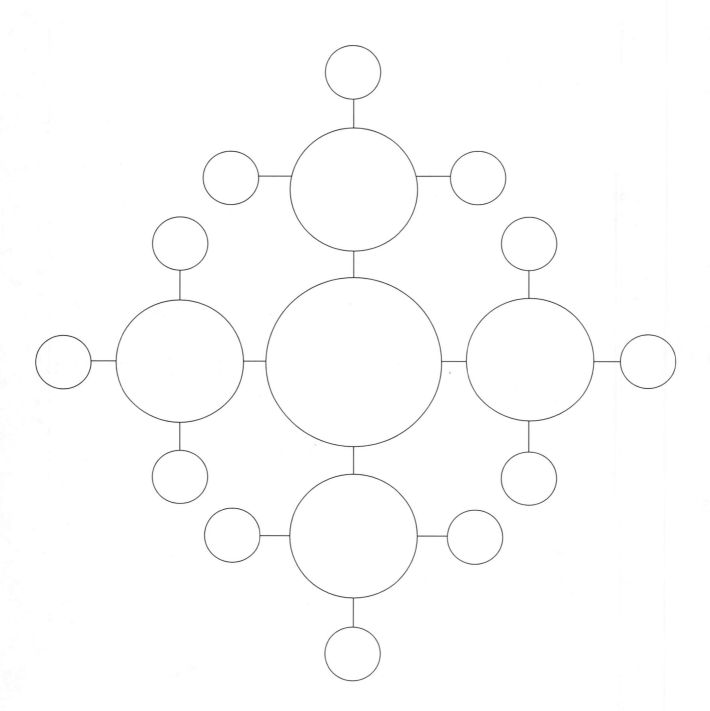

| | | | | |
|---|---|---|---|---|
| | | | | |
| | | | | |
| | | | | |
| | | | | |

A _____ is a _____ that
    (key word)          (description)

_____, _____, and
(characteristic)     (characteristic)

_____.
(characteristic)

relationship

_____ is to _____ [ ] as _____ is to _____.

relationship

_____ is to _____ [ ] as _____ is to _____.

relationship

_____ is to _____ [ ] as _____ is to _____.

relationship

_____ is to _____ [ ] as _____ is to _____.

relationship

_____ is to _____ [ ] as _____ is to _____.

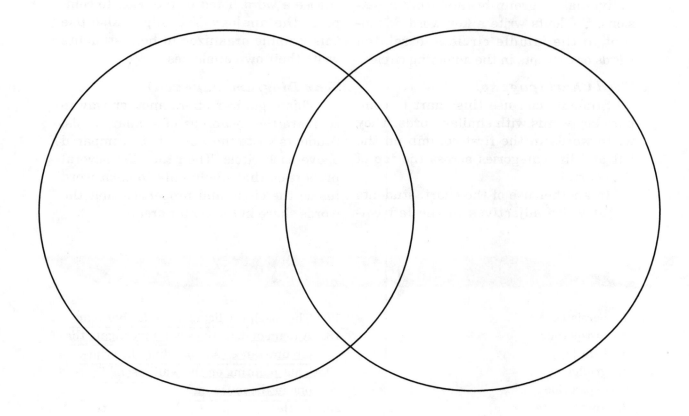

# USING THE GRAPHIC ORGANIZERS

**Understanding the Story (page xiii)**

This form will help students analyze the selection at the beginning of each unit and organize its content logically and visually.

**Cluster Map (page xiv)**

This organizer will help structure individual or group brainstorming sessions. Students write a key word or concept in the middle circle and related words or concepts in the adjoining circles.

**Word Chart (page xv)**

Students can use this chart to compare key words with similar words. They write words in the first column on the left and list categories across the top of the chart.

In another use of the chart, students might write adjectives in the left column. Across the top, they could list experiences.

**Analogy Organizer (page xvi)**

Students write in the box the relationship between the words in each pair. Then they write the three words given in the analogy in the blank spaces and choose a word listed in the book to complete the analogy. You might also use this graphic organizer to help students write their own analogies.

**Venn Diagram (page xvii)**

This organizer offers another way to compare the meanings of similar words. Students write the words to be compared above each circle. Then they list several properties that apply only to each word inside the circle and properties that the words share in the center area.

# Blue Test Answers

1. persisted
2. prosperous
3. frantic
4. grudge
5. expedition
6. appropriate
7. devoted
8. hoax
9. obligations
10. restored
11. schools
12. festivals
13. banquets
14. demonstrations
15. That company sells many different products.
16. The documentary described prison conditions in detail.
17. The coach predicted a win for her team.
18. A team of detectives will investigate the circumstances surrounding the crime.
19. That painting on the wall resembles one in the museum.
20. restless
21. cultural
22. monuments
23. breathtaking
24. binoculars
25. soared
26. stunned
27. perished
28. anguish
29. souvenirs

## WHAT DO THE WORDS MEAN?

>>>> *Following are some meanings, or definitions, for the ten vocabulary words in the box below. Write the words next to their definitions.*

| | | | | |
|---|---|---|---|---|
| frantic | appropriate | devoted | persisted | grudge |
| obligations | expedition | restored | prosperous | hoax |

1. _____ continued in spite of obstacles

2. _____ successful

3. _____ wild with excitement

4. _____ resentment; ill feelings

5. _____ a group of people undertaking a special journey

6. _____ proper

7. _____ gave up one's time, money or efforts for a cause

8. _____ a trick

9. _____ duties; responsibilities

10. _____ brought back to its original state; reconstructed

## FIND THE ANALOGIES

>>>> An **analogy** is a relationship between pairs of words. Here's one kind of analogy: *cook* is to *restaurant* as *nurse* is to *hospital*. In this relationship, the first word in each pair is a worker, and the second word in each pair describes where the person works. See if you can complete the following analogies. Circle the correct word or words.

11. **Auctioneers** are to **auctions** as **instructors** are to

    a. expeditions     b. schools     c. movies     d. stores

12. **Carpenters** are to **buildings** as **clowns** are to

    a. festivals     b. train stations     c. fire stations     d. construction sites

13. **Accountants** are to **offices** as **waiters** are to

    a. hospitals     b. banquets     c. schools     d. supermarkets

14. **Technicians** are to **laboratories** as **activists** are to

    a. concerts     b. movies     c. festivals     d. demonstrations

>>>> The **subject** of a sentence names the person, place, or thing that is spoken about. The **predicate** of a sentence is what is said about the subject. For example:   <u>The conductor waved his baton.</u> *The conductor* is the subject because it tells what the sentence is about. *Waved his baton* is the predicate because it tells what the conductor did.

*In the following sentences, draw one line under the subject and two lines under the predicate.*

**15.** That company sells many different products.

**16.** The documentary described prison conditions in detail.

**17.** The coach predicted a win for her team.

**18.** A team of detectives will investigate the circumstances surrounding the crime.

**19.** That painting on the wall resembles one in the museum.

## COMPLETE THE STORY

>>>> *Use words from the box to fill in the blanks and complete the story. Use each word only once.*

| | | | | |
|---|---|---|---|---|
| binoculars | breathtaking | cultural | perished | soared |
| monuments | restless | stunned | souvenirs | anguish |

Keith expected to be bored and **(20)** _____ during his class trip to Washington, D. C. He usually did not enjoy looking at **(21)** _____ exhibits or stone **(22)** _____. However, even Keith had to admit that the views of the White House, Capitol, and other buildings were **(23)** _____. He used his **(24)** _____ to get a closer look at the buildings that **(25)** _____ above him.

Keith was especially **(26)** _____ by the black wall with names of men and women who had **(27)** _____ in the Vietnam war. He could almost feel the **(28)** _____ of a woman who stood staring at a name on the wall. In the end, the trip turned out to be too short, and the **(29)** _____ Keith brought back just made him eager to go again.

# CONTENTS

Space Camp Launch

# 1 AN UNUSUAL CAMP

Do you feel *restless* here on Earth? Would you rather be flying in a space shuttle? If that sounds exciting, consider Space Camp.

In 1982, about 800 young people enrolled in the first Space Camp, located beside NASA's Marshall Space Flight Center in Huntsville, Alabama. In 1988, a second Space Camp opened near the Kennedy Space Center in Florida. Even then few people could have *predicted* the great success of this special camp.

Now 25,000 campers a year experience *intensive* training similar to what *actual* astronauts receive. Campers bounce off walls in nearly zero gravity and try out an apparatus that gives them the feeling of floating in outer space. Between these activity sessions, campers taste space food and learn about space travel from the camp *instructors.*

At the end of the week, one team of campers sits in an imitation Mission Control and directs the launch of a model space shuttle. Another team rides the model as it is launched and orbits Earth. The teams face frightening *circumstances* set up by their instructors. Some teams might have to deal with an *abrupt* loss of oxygen or engine failure, while others might have to avoid a *probable* crash with a meteor. The teams must not let their attention *falter.* They have to work within a slim *margin* of error to land the shuttle safely.

The idea behind Space Camp is to encourage young people's interest in space. It must be working because some of the first graduates of Space Camp are now in military academies, preparing to become astronauts. They plan to board real space shuttles someday soon. At Space Camp, they launched not only a shuttle but their careers.

## UNDERSTANDING THE STORY

>>>> *Circle the letter next to each correct statement.*

1. The statement that best expresses the main idea of this selection is that
   a. space travel can be frightening and dangerous.
   b. Space Camp helps young people learn more about flying space shuttles.
   c. Space Camp allows young people to experience space travel firsthand.

2. From this story, you can conclude that
   a. Space Camp strengthens young people's problem-solving skills.
   b. most space campers intend to become astronauts.
   c. astronauts who have attended Space Camp can skip some of the training they would usually receive.

# MAKE AN ALPHABETICAL LIST

>>>> *Here are the ten vocabulary words in this lesson. Write them in alphabetical order in the spaces below.*

| margin | instructors | predicted | circumstances | restless |
| abrupt | probable | intensive | actual | falter |

1. abrupt
2. actual
3. circumstances
4. falter
5. instructors

6. intensive
7. margin
8. predicted
9. probable
10. restless

# WHAT DO THE WORDS MEAN?

>>>> *Following are some meanings, or definitions, for the ten vocabulary words in this lesson. Write the words next to their definitions.*

1. restless — uneasy; bored

2. predicted — described what would happen in the future; forecasted

3. actual — real

4. probable — likely to happen

5. intensive — concentrated

6. falter — to hesitate; to fail or weaken

7. abrupt — sudden

8. instructors — teachers; leaders

9. circumstances — conditions

10. margin — a border; the space allowed for something

# FIND THE ANALOGIES

>>>> An **analogy** is a relationship between words. Here's one kind of analogy: *raindrop* is to *wet* as *sunlight* is to *hot*. In this relationship, the first word in each pair is an object and the second word in each pair describes the object.

>>>> *See if you can complete the following analogies. Circle the correct word or words.*

1. **Stop** is to **abrupt** as **camper** is to

  **a.** sudden        **b.** excited        **c.** predicted        **d.** intensive

2. **Training** is to **intensive** as **launch** is to

  **a.** actual        **b.** restless        **c.** complex        **d.** absorb

3. **Instructor** is to **patient** as **student** is to

  **a.** plural        **b.** medical        **c.** married        **d.** fascinated

4. **Death** is to **certain** as **marriage** is to

  **a.** probable        **b.** faltering        **c.** anxious        **d.** lonely

5. **Wages** is to **calculated** as **weather** is to

  **a.** autumn        **b.** predicted        **c.** vacation        **d.** winter

# USE YOUR OWN WORDS

>>>> *Look at the picture. What words come into your mind other than the ten vocabulary words used in this lesson? Write them on the lines below. To help you get started, here are two good words:*

1.      realistic
2.      exciting
3.      Answers will vary.
4. 
5. 
6. 
7. 
8. 
9. 
10. 

# FIND THE ADJECTIVES

>>>> An **adjective** is a word that describes a person, place, or thing. The adjectives in the following sentences are underlined: The <u>excited</u> campers cheered (person). They slept in a <u>new</u> dormitory (place). The <u>enormous</u> engines began to roar (thing).

>>>> *Underline the adjectives in the following sentences.*

**1.** Teams must prepare for <u>abrupt</u> changes in the weather.

**2.** The leader had a suggestion for his <u>restless</u> team.

**3.** <u>Good</u> instructors are important for a <u>successful</u> <u>camping</u> experience.

**4.** The <u>team</u> members knew they had a <u>narrow</u> margin of safety.

**5.** <u>Intensive</u> training paid off as the <u>huge</u> shuttle was launched.

# COMPLETE THE STORY

>>>> Here are the ten vocabulary words for this lesson:

| | | | | |
|---|---|---|---|---|
| margin | restless | abrupt | predicted | instructors |
| probable | circumstances | actual | falter | intensive |

>>>> *There are six blank spaces in the story below. Four vocabulary words have already been used in the story. They are underlined. Use the other six words to fill in the blanks.*

Space Camp _____instructors_____ give the campers _____intensive_____ training before they fly the space shuttle. The campers are warned not to get _____restless_____ or let their attention <u>falter</u> for a second. The campers discuss with the instructors the <u>probable</u> obstacles they may face and how to deal with them.

Even though campers know they are pretending, the equipment and computer screens make the <u>circumstances</u> seem real. They prepare for an _____actual_____ shuttle launch and flight. They know they have a slim <u>margin</u> for error. They realize that not all problems can be _____predicted_____ ahead of time. The teams understand that mistakes can lead to an _____abrupt_____ crash or explosion of the shuttle.

## Learn More About Space Travel

>>>> *On a separate sheet of paper or in your notebook or journal, complete one or more of the activities below.*

### Learning Across the Curriculum

Research how living in zero gravity can affect human muscles, especially the heart. Write a short report describing the problems involved and actions astronauts might take to avoid these problems.

### Learning Across the Curriculum

Find out how cuts in the federal budget have affected plans for building a space station or revisiting the moon. Then write a proposal suggesting either how to raise more money or what parts of the space program the government should focus on with limited funds.

### Broadening Your Understanding

Invite someone who has been to Space Camp to talk with your class about his or her experiences. Or watch a videotape of the movie *Space Camp*. Discuss which parts of the movie plot you think could come true and which parts seemed to be fiction.

# 2 DYNAMIC BETTE

The young woman stood before the curtain in the Palace Theater in New York City, her head bowed. The `frantic` applause of the audience brought tears to her eyes. Bette Midler's `debut` at the Palace Theater was a tremendous success.

This setting was very different from the gentle, rolling hills of Aiea, a small town near the city of Honolulu, Hawaii, where Bette Midler was born. Midler's `aptitude` for music and acting led her into her profession—show business. She came to the mainland and became a member of an acting group that performed for children. Later, in order to support herself, Midler worked in the coatroom of a nightclub. One day a friend suggested that Midler `apply` for a role in a play. The producers liked Midler and later gave her an important role in the musical *Fiddler on the Roof.*

Although she started her career as an actress, Midler first became famous as a pop singer. She received `ovations` for her `dynamic` stage presence and her `renditions` of both old and new songs. Later she decided to return to acting. In *The Rose,* a film about a rock singer, Midler firmly established her credentials as a `skillful` actress. From there, she progressed to films, such as *Ruthless People, Outrageous Fortune, Beaches,* and *For the Boys.* She also had a starring role in the television movie *Gypsy.* Today she is one of the most popular actresses in Hollywood.

Critics `commend` her performances on the stage and screen. Fans the world over `clamor` for more from Bette Midler.

## UNDERSTANDING THE STORY

>>>> *Circle the letter next to each correct statement.*

1. The main idea of this story is to
   a. describe the place where Bette Midler was born.
   b. tell the reader about some of the events in Midler's career.
   c. encourage young singers to imitate Midler's style.

2. From this story, you can conclude that
   a. Bette Midler was born into show business.
   b. Midler never really liked acting on the stage.
   c. luck, talent, and hard work have all contributed to Midler's success.

9

# MAKE AN ALPHABETICAL LIST

>>>> *Here are the ten vocabulary words in this lesson. Write them in alphabetical order in the spaces below.*

| frantic | renditions | clamor | commend | dynamic |
| ovations | aptitude | debut | skillful | apply |

1. apply
2. aptitude
3. clamor
4. commend
5. debut
6. dynamic
7. frantic
8. ovations
9. renditions
10. skillful

# WHAT DO THE WORDS MEAN?

>>>> *Following are some meanings, or definitions, for the ten vocabulary words in this lesson. Write the words next to their definitions.*

1. frantic — wild with excitement; out of control

2. debut — a first appearance before the public

3. aptitude — a natural ability or capacity; a talent

4. dynamic — full of energy; vigorous

5. apply — to seek a job; to ask for work

6. renditions — performances or interpretations

7. skillful — having ability gained by practice or knowledge; expert

8. ovations — bursts of loud clapping or cheering; waves of applause

9. commend — to praise; to acclaim as worthy of notice

10. clamor — to demand noisily; to call for loudly

# COMPLETE THE SENTENCES

>>>> *Use the vocabulary words in this lesson to complete the following sentences. Use each word only once.*

| dynamic | aptitude | ovations | renditions | apply |
|---------|----------|----------|------------|-------|
| frantic | skillful | commend | debut | clamor |

1. Standing ___ovations___ are the dream of many young entertainers.

2. Midler's audiences grew to expect ___dynamic___ performances.

3. Midler's ___renditions___ of songs always thrill her audiences.

4. Before Midler made her ___debut___, she worked small jobs.

5. Many people ___apply___ for each part in a play, but only a few are chosen.

6. There is a ___frantic___ search for a replacement when the star of a show gets sick.

7. Bette Midler has a rare ___aptitude___ for both comedy and song.

8. No one expected the critics to ___commend___ Midler's performance in the movie *The Rose,* but they all gave it rave reviews.

9. Midler is ___skillful___ at relaxing her audience.

10. Fans stand and ___clamor___ for more at the end of Midler's performances.

# USE YOUR OWN WORDS

>>>> *Look at the picture. What words come into your mind other than the ten vocabulary words used in this lesson? Write them on the lines below. To help you get started, here are two good words:*

1. ___costumes___
2. ___bunny___
3. ___Answers will vary.___
4. _____
5. _____
6. _____
7. _____
8. _____
9. _____
10. _____

# FIND THE SUBJECTS AND PREDICATES

>>>> The **subject** of a sentence names the person, place, or thing that is spoken about. The **predicate** of a sentence is what is said about the subject. For example:

> The small boy went to the football game.

*The small boy* is the subject (the person the sentence is talking about). *Went to the football game* is the predicate of the sentence (because it tells what the small boy did).

>>>> *In the following sentences, draw one line under the subject of the sentence and two lines under the predicate of the sentence.*

1. The young woman stood before the curtain.

2. Bette Midler was born in Aiea, Hawaii.

3. Midler became famous as a singer.

4. Critics commended all Midler's performances.

5. Midler performs on the stage and screen.

# COMPLETE THE STORY

>>>> Here are the ten vocabulary words for this lesson:

| | | | | |
|---|---|---|---|---|
| frantic | apply | debut | clamor | aptitude |
| skillful | dynamic | commend | renditions | ovations |

>>>> *There are six blank spaces in the story below. Four vocabulary words have already been used in the story. They are underlined. Use the other six words to fill in the blanks.*

In order to become a <u>dynamic</u> performer, one must first have the ___aptitude___ necessary to be successful. One must be able to give good ___renditions___ of many types of songs. A ___skillful___ use of talent and an ability to <u>apply</u> oneself to rigid schedules help to bring fame. <u>Frantic</u> applause of the audience can greet a ___debut___ on the stage. Standing ___ovations___ will be given to these artists at every concert.

Fans will always ___clamor___ for more music from their favorite artists, and critics will <u>commend</u> notable performances.

## Learn More About Popular Singers

>>>> *On a separate sheet of paper or in your notebook or journal, complete one or more of the activities below.*

### Learning Across the Curriculum

All cultures have a celebrity like a Bette Midler—a singer who is larger than life. Think about a singer who performs in another language. Listen to one of his or her recordings and to a recording by Bette Midler. Compare the two singers. Would each be popular in the other one's country? Why or why not?

### Broadening Your Understanding

Bette Midler's talent as an actress and a singer make her a natural for musicals like *Fiddler on the Roof*. Watch a musical on video. When you have finished, write a review describing your opinion of the performance. Share your report with the class.

### Extending your Reading

Read one of these biographies of popular singers, or find a biography of a singer whom you want to learn more about. Now imagine you are writing a movie about this singer's life. Use the events in the singer's life to create the outline for a movie.

*Elvis Presley: The King,* by Katherine Krohn
*Paula Abdul: Straight Up,* by Ford Thomas
*Gloria Estefan,* by Rebecca Stefoff
*Whitney Houston,* by Keith Elli Greenberg

The challenge of climbing a mountain has attracted brave people. Many have failed. Some have been forced to give up. Others have fallen to their deaths or perished in severe blizzards.

Climbing Mount Everest has always been the mountaineer's dream. Towering 29,028 feet above sea level, the summit of Mount Everest stands higher than any other. Located in the Himalaya Mountains, this icy peak is one of the greatest challenges on Earth.

Edmund Hillary was determined to scale this mountain. With his native guide Tenzing, he called together a group of hardy mountaineers. Top physical condition was needed for this perilous journey.

Hillary led the way with his guide and climbing companion. For a while, the expedition went smoothly and without any problems. He warned the other mountaineers about these hidden chasms.

Suddenly a snow ledge gave way, and Hillary fell. Tenzing slammed his pickax into the face of the ice-covered mountain, grabbed the life rope, dug in his heels, and held on. The falling man slowly came to a stop on the sheer face of the cliff. He was saved by a thin rope and a brave friend.

For a moment, Hillary had come close to death. But the hardy band of mountaineers continued their climb. Finally, they attained their goal. As the first to reach the summit of Mount Everest, they had made the mountaineer's dream come true.

## UNDERSTANDING THE STORY

>>>> *Circle the letter next to each correct statement.*

1. When asked why he wanted to climb Mount Everest, a famous mountaineer replied, "Because it is there." He meant that
   a. there wasn't a mountain he couldn't climb.
   b. the challenge of conquering a mountain was reason enough.
   c. even if he failed, the mountain would still be there.

2. For a person to climb a mountain, such as Mount Everest, successfully, the climber must
   a. have great confidence in the bravery and skill of the other climbers on the expedition.
   b. spend millions of dollars on equipment and supplies.
   c. study in great detail the maps used by Edmund Hillary.

# MAKE AN ALPHABETICAL LIST

>>>> *Here are the ten vocabulary words in this lesson. Write them in alphabetical order in the spaces below.*

| | | | | |
|---|---|---|---|---|
| challenge | summit | perished | scale | hardy |
| attained | expedition | perilous | chasms | sheer |

1. attained
2. challenge
3. chasms
4. expedition
5. hardy

6. perilous
7. perished
8. scale
9. sheer
10. summit

# WHAT DO THE WORDS MEAN?

>>>> *Following are some meanings, or definitions, for the ten vocabulary words in this lesson. Write the words next to their definitions.*

1. expedition — a group of people undertaking a special journey, such as mountain climbing

2. sheer — steep; straight up and down

3. chasms — deep openings or cracks

4. attained — reached; achieved

5. perished — died, usually in a violent manner

6. summit — the peak; the highest point

7. challenge — a call to a contest or battle

8. perilous — dangerous; hazardous

9. hardy — able to take hard physical treatment; bold; daring

10. scale — to climb

# COMPLETE THE SENTENCES

>>>> *Use the vocabulary words in this lesson to complete the following sentences. Use each word only once.*

| | | | | |
|---|---|---|---|---|
| hardy | scale | perilous | challenge | chasms |
| expedition | summit | perished | sheer | attained |

1. Before the ____expedition____ could leave, years of planning were necessary.

2. Some people cannot resist the ____challenge____ of climbing a huge mountain.

3. The ____sheer____ face of the cliff, slowed the mountaineers' progress.

4. The lead climbers had a good chance to ____scale____ the cliff.

5. Only a very ____hardy____ person can stand the freezing temperatures.

6. Because the climb was ____perilous____, the climbers took safety precautions.

7. They had to watch out for ____chasms____ in the mountain walls.

8. Only three people reached the ____summit____, although the others almost did.

9. The group had ____attained____ its goal, but at the terrible cost of two lives.

10. In memory of the climbers who had ____perished____, they erected a stone marker.

# USE YOUR OWN WORDS

>>>> *Look at the picture. What words come into your mind other than the ten vocabulary words used in this lesson? Write them on the lines below. To help you get started, here are two good words:*

1. _____steep_____
2. _____snow_____
3. ____Answers will vary.____
4. _____
5. _____
6. _____
7. _____
8. _____
9. _____
10. _____

# DESCRIBE THE NOUNS

>>>> *Two of the vocabulary words, summit and expedition, are nouns. List as many words as you can that describe or tell something about the words summit and expedition. You can work on this with your classmates. Listed below are some words to help you get started.*
Answers may vary.

| **summit** | **expedition** |
|---|---|
| 1. high | 1. large |
| 2. cold | 2. careful |
| 3. freezing | 3. skilled |
| 4. icy | 4. trained |
| 5. windy | 5. prepared |
| 6. lonely | 6. organized |
| 7. isolated | 7. unusual |
| 8. dangerous | 8. fearful |

# COMPLETE THE STORY

>>>> Here are the ten vocabulary words for this lesson:

| | | | | |
|---|---|---|---|---|
| challenge | summit | perished | scale | hardy |
| attained | expedition | perilous | chasms | sheer |

>>>> *There are six blank spaces in the story below. Four vocabulary words have already been used in the story. They are underlined. Use the other six words to fill in the blanks.*

There are many high mountain peaks in the world that offer a great
_____challenge_____ to mountaineers. For centuries, men and women have tried to
_____scale_____ their heights. The _____hardy_____ leader of an
expedition must gather together the best mountaineers and equipment. They must
plan every step of the way in order to achieve their goal. Despite their great skill and
bravery, many mountaineers have perished. Some have slipped on the
_____sheer_____ face of a cliff and fallen into deep chasms. Others have died in
blizzards on their _____perilous_____ journey. When an expedition reaches the
summit, there is great joy. The climbers have _____attained_____ their goal of
conquering a mountain.

## Learn More About the Himalayas

>>>> *On a separate sheet of paper or in your notebook or journal, complete one or more of the activities below.*

### Learning Across the Curriculum

The Himalaya Mountains, which include Mount Everest, are one of the most impressive mountain ranges in the world. Find out how this mountain range was formed. Then draw a series of illustrations that explain the process that created the Himalayas.

### Broadening Your Understanding

Hillary's native guide Tenzing was a Sherpa. Without Tenzing, Hillary would not have been able to reach the summit of Everest. Find out more about these people of the Himalayas. Write what you find about them. What do they eat? What language do they speak? How do they survive in the harsh land of the Himalayas?

### Extending Your Reading

Big Foot, the Abominable Snowman or yeti, is said to come from the Himalayas. Read the information on this monster in one of the books below. Then write about whether you believe the Abominable Snowman really exists.

*Big Foot,* by Ruth Shannon Odor
*The Abominable Snowman,* by Barbara Antonopolos
*Stranger Than Fiction: Monsters,* by Melvin Berger

When Walter Dean Myers was growing up in New York's Harlem, little children sang and held hands on their way to Sunday school. As these happy children became teenagers, however, they also became discouraged by the *barriers* facing them. Myers himself *flirted* with gangs and drugs, but he was rescued by his love of reading and writing.

Myers was born in 1937 and was *informally* adopted by Florence and Herbert Dean when he was 3. They taught him to read when he was a *mere* 4 years old. Despite his ability, school was *misery.* Myers lashed out at classmates who teased him because of a speech problem. Soon officials were trying to suspend the angry and *sullen* boy from school—permanently.

Myers *dealt* with rejection by staying home and reading. He was absent from school so much that he showed up one day without realizing that summer vacation had begun! Then he started to hang out on the streets. Partly to escape a death threat from a gang, Myers joined the Army in 1954 on his 17th birthday.

It was not until 1977 that Myers became a full-time writer. He has helped to *define* life in today's cities through more than a dozen *novels.* The young people in his stories face despair and struggle for ways to survive. Through his characters, Myers explores friendship, responsibility, and self-discovery.

His many awards include the 1988 Newbery Honor Book Award for the *publication* of *Scorpions*. Myers's strong dialogue and his combination of humor and hope make his books very popular with young people.

## UNDERSTANDING THE STORY

>>>> *Circle the letter next to each correct statement.*

1. The statement that best expresses the main idea of this selection is that
   **a.** Myers has used his own experiences to write stories that seem very real.
   **b.** as a teenager, Myers narrowly escaped becoming involved with gangs.
   **c.** Myers's speech problems kept him from doing well at school.

2. From this story, you can conclude that
   **a.** Walter Dean Myers no longer lives in Harlem.
   **b.** Myers would tell beginning writers to focus on what they are familiar with.
   **c.** Myers always wanted to be a writer.

# MAKE AN ALPHABETICAL LIST

>>>> *Here are the ten vocabulary words in this lesson. Write them in alphabetical order in the spaces below.*

| | | | | |
|---|---|---|---|---|
| publication | flirted | dealt | define | novels |
| informally | misery | mere | sullen | barriers |

1. barriers
2. dealt
3. define
4. flirted
5. informally

6. mere
7. misery
8. novels
9. publication
10. sullen

# WHAT DO THE WORDS MEAN?

>>>> *Following are some meanings, or definitions, for the ten vocabulary words in this lesson. Write the words next to their definitions.*

1. novels — long stories about imaginary people and events

2. sullen — gloomy; resentful

3. barriers — obstacles; walls

4. dealt — handled; managed; faced

5. informally — a way of doing something that does not follow exact rules or procedures; casually

6. flirted — showed an interest

7. misery — suffering; distress

8. define — to explain the meaning of

9. mere — only; barely

10. publication — the production of written material into printed form

# FIND THE ANALOGIES

>>>> An **analogy** is a relationship between words. Here's one kind of analogy: *barber* is to *haircut* as *farmer* is to *corn*. In this relationship, the first word in each pair is a worker, and the second word in each pair is the worker's product.

>>>> *See if you can complete the following analogies. Circle the correct word or words.*

1. **Police officer** is to **safety** as **author** is to
   **a.** handcuffs **b.** paper **c.** novels **d.** computers

2. **Teacher** is to **learning** as **construction worker** is to
   **a.** a building **b.** a bulldozer **c.** cement **d.** misery

3. **Dentist** is to **healthy teeth** as **doctor** is to
   **a.** injections **b.** good health **c.** medicine **d.** appointment

4. **Salesperson** is to **sale** as **typist** is to
   **a.** office **b.** letters **c.** barriers **d.** define

5. **Truck driver** is to **transporting goods** as **plumber** is to
   **a.** pipe wrench **b.** emergency call **c.** fixing pipes **d.** drains

# USE YOUR OWN WORDS

>>>> *Look at the picture. What words come into your mind other than the ten vocabulary words used in this lesson? Write them on the lines below. To help you get started, here are two good words:*

1. _____dramatic_____
2. _____exciting_____
3. ___Answers will vary.___
4. _____
5. _____
6. _____
7. _____
8. _____
9. _____
10. _____

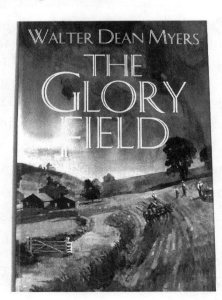

WALTER DEAN MYERS
THE GLORY FIELD

# UNSCRAMBLE THE LETTERS

>>>> *Each group of letters represents one of the vocabulary words for this lesson. Can you unscramble them? Write your answers in the blanks on the right.*

| Scrambled Letters | Vocabulary Words |
|---|---|
| 1. slenul | sullen |
| 2. finallymor | informally |
| 3. lovens | novels |
| 4. myries | misery |
| 5. reem | mere |
| 6. driftel | flirted |
| 7. bilioncaput | publication |
| 8. atled | dealt |
| 9. sribarer | barriers |
| 10. fededin | defined |

# COMPLETE THE STORY

>>>> Here are the ten vocabulary words for this lesson:

| | | | | |
|---|---|---|---|---|
| novels | misery | barriers | flirted | mere |
| sullen | define | publication | dealt | informally |

>>>> *There are six blank spaces in the story below. Four vocabulary words have already been used in the story. They are underlined. Use the other six words to fill in the blanks.*

When you talk <u>informally</u> with friends about books, do you discuss
_____novels_____ or nonfiction? People <u>define</u> a book of nonfiction as a
_____publication_____ that is true and based on facts. When you are assigned a book
report at school, do you feel joy or _____misery_____? Some students look <u>sullen</u>
when they are asked to read a book they do not find interesting. They may spend a
_____mere_____ hour or less skimming the book.

However, young people want to read Walter Dean Myers's books because they are
about teenagers who have _____flirted_____ with danger and even death. Some of
his characters have _____dealt_____ with major hardships and <u>barriers</u>. They
have found ways to survive and even to succeed.

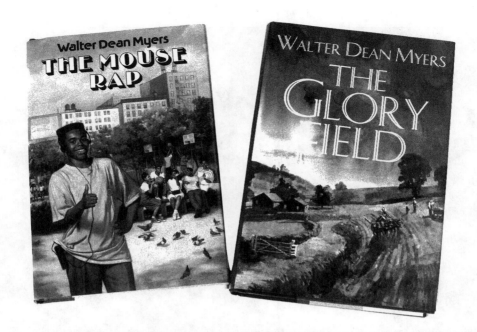

## Learn More About Writers

>>>> *On a separate sheet of paper or in your notebook or journal, complete one or more of the activities below.*

### Learning Across the Curriculum

Write a short story or create some kind of visual art based on your own childhood memories and experiences. If you wish, share your work with a partner or a small group.

### Broadening Your Understanding

Read a novel by an author you enjoy. Then, based on the novel, write an essay on how you think the author's childhood experiences may have influenced the story.

### Extending Your Reading

Choose one of the following books by Walter Dean Myers. After reading the book, explain how the story might change if it had a different setting. For example, suppose the main characters lived or grew up in the suburbs or a farming community instead of the city. How might their lives and their problems change? What parts of the story might stay the same?

*Glory Field*
*The Mouse Rap*
*Fast Sam, Cool Clyde, and Stuff*
*Hoops*
*It Ain't All for Nothin'*
*Somewhere in the Darkness*
*Motown and Didi*
*Scorpions*
*The Young Landlords*

Although this city has been invaded and destroyed or partly destroyed more than 40 times, it has always been rebuilt. Ruin has been piled upon ruin until today the streets are 35 feet higher than they were 2,000 years ago.

For ages, Jerusalem has been a $\boxed{sacred}$ city. It is the center of three $\boxed{religious}$ groups—the Jews, the Christians, and the Muslims. For this reason, Jerusalem has been called the land of the star, the cross, and the $\boxed{crescent.}$ Each of these three $\boxed{symbols}$ stands for one of the three religions. The star is the Star of David for the Jewish religion. The cross is the cross of Jesus for the Christian religion. The crescent is the symbol for the Muslim religion.

Jerusalem is divided into two parts—the old city and the new city. The new Jerusalem $\boxed{resembles}$ a modern city. It has tall buildings and crowded streets. The old Jerusalem has hardly changed during its long history. Many of the towers and religious $\boxed{shrines}$ that were built long ago still stand.

The clothes worn by the people of Jerusalem also $\boxed{reflect}$ the old and the new. Some people wear the $\boxed{apparel}$ of their $\boxed{forebears.}$ Others dress in the latest styles.

New and old, Jews, Christians, and Muslims, all $\boxed{mingle}$ in the narrow streets of Jerusalem. Both the beauty and importance of this great city have made it "Jerusalem the Golden."

## UNDERSTANDING THE STORY

 *Circle the letter next to each correct statement.*

1. The main idea of this story is that
   a. Jerusalem is a city torn by wars and in need of rebuilding.
   b. Jerusalem is a mix of the old and the new, and its people are a mix of different faiths.
   c. symbols are necessary to tell religions apart.

2. From this story, you can conclude that
   a. millions of people have strong emotional ties to Jerusalem.
   b. the days of the destruction of Jerusalem are over.
   c. people in the new part of the city are more religious than people in the old part.

# MAKE AN ALPHABETICAL LIST

>>>> *Here are the ten vocabulary words in this lesson. Write them in alphabetical order in the spaces below.*

| sacred | religious | crescent | symbols | shrines |
| resembles | apparel | reflect | forebears | mingle |

1. apparel
2. crescent
3. forebears
4. mingle
5. reflect

6. religious
7. resembles
8. sacred
9. shrines
10. symbols

# WHAT DO THE WORDS MEAN?

>>>> *Following are some meanings, or definitions, for the ten vocabulary words in this lesson. Write the words next to their definitions.*

1. sacred — holy; worthy of reverence

2. crescent — the shape of the moon in the first or last quarter; the symbol of the Muslim religion

3. symbols — things that stand for or represent something else; signs

4. religious — having to do with a belief in God; devout

5. resembles — looks like; is similar in appearance

6. shrines — sacred places; places where holy things are kept

7. reflect — to give back an image of

8. apparel — clothing; dress

9. forebears — family members who lived a long time ago

10. mingle — to mix; to get along together

# COMPLETE THE SENTENCES

>>>> *Use the vocabulary words in this lesson to complete the following sentences. Use each word only once.*

| | | | | |
|---|---|---|---|---|
| shrines | apparel | resembles | symbols | religious |
| crescent | sacred | mingle | reflect | forebears |

1. Jerusalem is a city that has ___religious___ meaning for people of different faiths.

2. In buildings that were used by their ___forebears___, the people worship daily.

3. Throughout Jerusalem, one sees three famous ___symbols___—the star, the cross, and the crescent.

4. The ___crescent___ is a symbol that has special meaning for the Muslim people.

5. The Western Wall is a structure that is ___sacred___ to the Jewish people.

6. The religious ___shrines___ in the old city are visited by people from far and near.

7. People of different races, religions, and styles ___mingle___ in the streets.

8. To judge by the ___apparel___ worn by some of the people in the old city, there has been little change over the centuries.

9. However, the new part of Jerusalem ___resembles___ most other modern cities.

10. The tall buildings in new Jerusalem ___reflect___ the modern tastes of people in that section of the city.

# USE YOUR OWN WORDS

>>>> *Look at the picture. What words come into your mind other than the ten vocabulary words used in this lesson? Write them on the lines below. To help you get started, here are two good words:*

1. ___dome___
2. ___trucks___
3. ___Answers will vary.___
4. _____
5. _____
6. _____
7. _____
8. _____
9. _____
10. _____

# FIND THE ANALOGIES

>>>> In an **analogy,** similar relationships occur between words that are different. For example, *pig* is to *hog* as *car* is to *automobile.* The relationship is that the words mean the same. Here's another analogy: *noisy* is to *quiet* as *short* is to *tall.* In this relationship, the words have opposite meanings.

>>>> *See if you can complete the following analogies. Circle the correct word or words.*

1. **Crescent** is to **Muslim** as **star** is to
   **a.** sky          **b.** Christian          **c.** astronaut          **d.** Jewish *(circled)*

2. **Holy** is to **sacred** as **devout** is to
   **a.** man          **b.** child          **c.** religious *(circled)*          **d.** shrines

3. **Knowledge** is to **ignorance** as **mingle** is to
   **a.** mix          **b.** together          **c.** separate *(circled)*          **d.** truth

4. **Apparel** is to **body** as **shoe** is to
   **a.** shine          **b.** laces          **c.** leather          **d.** foot *(circled)*

5. **Sacred** is to **unholy** as **up** is to
   **a.** planes          **b.** down *(circled)*          **c.** sad          **d.** planets

# COMPLETE THE STORY

>>>> Here are the ten vocabulary words for this lesson:

| | | | | |
|---|---|---|---|---|
| sacred | religious | crescent | symbols | shrines |
| resembles | apparel | reflect | forebears | mingle |

>>>> *There are six blank spaces in the story below. Four vocabulary words have already been used in the story. They are underlined. Use the other six words to fill in the blanks.*

Within old Jerusalem are three famous _____shrines_____ that have been sacred to Christians, Jews, and Muslims for many centuries. While new Jerusalem _____resembles_____ any other modern city, the old city of the star, the cross, and the crescent has changed very little. These symbols _____reflect_____ the many influences upon this city.

Its narrow, winding streets are filled with people wearing the same kind of _____apparel_____ that their forebears wore. Many very _____religious_____ people of different traditions meet and _____mingle_____ with one another. If you visit this city, you can't help being touched by its history and culture.

## Learn More About the Middle East

>>>> *On a separate sheet of paper or in your notebook or journal, complete one or more of the activities below.*

### Appreciating Diversity

Learn more about a large city in another country. Research what it is like and write a report. You may want to illustrate your report with your own art.

### Broadening Your Understanding

Find out more about what tourists go to see in Jerusalem. Then read more about these sights. Now imagine you have just been to visit Jerusalem. Write a postcard to a friend at home explaining the most interesting sight. Draw a picture of what you saw for the front of the postcard.

### Learning Across the Curriculum

Read the newspaper and find an article about the Middle East. Find more about the issue the newspaper article is addressing. Then write a summary of what you learn.

# 6 A BASEBALL LEGEND

As a small boy in Puerto Rico, Roberto Clemente dreamed of playing baseball. He did not plan to become one of the most admired players in history. He just wanted to play the game he loved so much.

One day, a baseball scout from the United States recognized young Clemente's great athletic skill. He took Clemente to the United States, where the young man ended up playing for the Pittsburgh Pirates. At first, Clemente experienced *prejudice* because of his skin color and his *cultural* background. He also had problems speaking English.

Clemente was proud to be Puerto Rican, however, and made no *apology* for his background. *Despite* insults from a few people, Clemente did not carry a *grudge.* He *persisted* in doing his best and helped the Pirates win the 1960 and 1971 World Series. He also earned four National League batting titles and was twice voted Most Valuable Player. Clemente's amazing skill brought him fame and admiration.

Still, this *recognition* did not make Clemente forget his *obligations* to his fans. For example, after winning the 1960 World Series, Clemente went back to the field to hug his delighted fans. Someone once gave Clemente $6,000. He donated it to Children's Hospital in Pittsburgh.

Clemente's concern for the *welfare* of others led to his death. In 1972, a strong earthquake left thousands in Nicaragua dead, hurt, or homeless. Clemente was in *anguish* over the situation. He decided to fly food and supplies to Nicaragua. Shortly after taking off, the plane plunged into the sea with Clemente aboard. No one survived.

Clemente is remembered not just as a baseball superstar, but also as a great and caring man.

## UNDERSTANDING THE STORY

>>>> *Circle the letter next to each correct statement.*

1. The statement that best expresses the main idea of this selection is that
   a. Clemente became famous and successful, and he reached out and helped others.
   b. Clemente helped others in order to draw attention to himself.
   c. Clemente was wrong to care about others.

2. From this story, you can conclude that
   a. Clemente's family encouraged him to be a baseball superstar.
   b. Clemente was ashamed of his background.
   c. Clemente did not mind when fans asked for his autograph.

# MAKE AN ALPHABETICAL LIST

>>>> *Here are the ten vocabulary words in this lesson. Write them in alphabetical order in the spaces below.*

| | | | | |
|---|---|---|---|---|
| recognition | welfare | despite | persisted | grudge |
| apology | anguish | obligations | prejudice | cultural |

1. anguish
2. apology
3. cultural
4. despite
5. grudge

6. obligations
7. persisted
8. prejudice
9. recognition
10. welfare

# WHAT DO THE WORDS MEAN?

>>>> *Following are some meanings, or definitions, for the ten vocabulary words in this lesson. Write the words next to their definitions.*

1. apology — an expression of regret for wrongdoing

2. welfare — happiness; well being

3. grudge — resentment; ill feelings

4. anguish — pain; sorrow

5. persisted — continued in spite of obstacles

6. recognition — special notice or attention

7. prejudice — dislike of people who are different

8. obligations — duties; responsibilities

9. despite — not prevented by; in spite of

10. cultural — relating to the beliefs and behaviors of a social, ethnic, or religious group

# FIND THE ANALOGIES

>>>> An **analogy** is a relationship between words. Here's one kind of analogy: *rain* is to *flood* as *sun* is to *burn*. In this relationship, the first word in each pair is the cause and the second word in each pair is the effect.

>>>> *See if you can complete the following analogies. Circle the correct word or words.*

1. **Grudge** is to **resentment** as **failure** is to

   **a.** ambition    **(b.)** disappointment    **c.** contentment    **d.** attempt

2. **Winning** is to **recognition** as **practicing** is to

   **(a.)** improvement    **b.** awards    **c.** failure    **d.** giving up

3. A **hard decision** is to **anguish** as a **funny movie** is to

   **a.** sorrow    **b.** nail biting    **(c.)** laughter    **d.** crying

4. A **job** is to **obligations** as **a day off** is to

   **(a.)** relaxation    **b.** responsibility    **c.** tension    **d.** resentment

5. **Making a mistake** is to **apology** as **receiving help** is to

   **a.** forgiven    **b.** anguish    **c.** congratulations    **(d.)** thanks

# USE YOUR OWN WORDS

>>>> *Look at the picture. What words come into your mind other than the ten vocabulary words used in this lesson? Write them on the blank lines below. To help you get started, here are two good words:*

1. admiration
2. caring
3. Answers will vary.
4. _____
5. _____
6. _____
7. _____
8. _____
9. _____
10. _____

**35**

## DESCRIBE THE NOUNS

>>>> *Two of the vocabulary words, obligations and anguish, are nouns. List as many words as you can that describe or tell something about the words obligations and anguish. You can work on this with your classmates.*

### obligations

1. _____
2. _____
3. _____
4. _____
5. _____
6. _____
7. _____
8. _____
9. _____
10. _____

### anguish

1. _____
2. _____
3. _____
4. _____
5. _____
6. _____
7. _____
8. _____
9. _____
10. _____

## COMPLETE THE STORY

>>>> Here are the ten vocabulary words for this lesson:

| apology | despite | welfare | grudge | obligations |
|---------|---------|---------|--------|-------------|
| anguish | cultural | recognition | prejudice | persisted |

>>>> *There are six blank spaces in the story below. Four vocabulary words have already been used in the story. They are underlined. Use the other six words to fill in the blanks.*

Many athletes have faced _____prejudice_____ because of their <u>cultural</u> backgrounds. Some carry a _____grudge_____ throughout their careers. Others put aside their <u>anguish</u> and win respect and _____recognition_____ with their athletic skill. <u>Despite</u> the fact that some fans insulted him, Roberto Clemente continued to care about the _____welfare_____ of all people.

Even when he was famous and popular, he felt he had <u>obligations</u> to others. He _____persisted_____ in reaching out to people in trouble. Clemente never needed to make an _____apology_____ for the way he led his short life.

## Learn More About Sports

>>>> *On a separate sheet of paper or in your notebook or journal, complete one or more of the activities below.*

### Building Language

Explain at least two meanings for each of these words: *fan, sport, field*. Use each word in two sentences to show the different meanings.

### Learning Across the Curriculum

Write a short report about another sports star who is admired for his or her contributions outside of sports. Choose two names from the list below. Share what you learn with the class.

Wilma Rudolph
Bill Bradley
Arthur Ashe
Jackie Joyner-Kersee
José Torres

### Broadening Your Understanding

In a short report, compare Roberto Clemente with one of today's baseball players. How are their attitudes toward playing baseball and toward their fans similar? How are they different? How would you explain the differences in their attitudes?

# 7 A NEW KIND OF COUNTRY

Country songs often tell of somebody's troubles. When Randy Travis sings, the words have real meaning for him. He was born near Marshville, North Carolina. His family worked hard, but his father urged his boys to take up the guitar. Travis practiced and gave his first performance at the age of eight.

But Travis got into trouble. He dropped out of school in the ninth grade. He argued with his parents and was in constant conflict. He was even arrested five times for drug- and drink-related incidents. Today he shrugs and says, "Now, I wouldn't have the ignorance or the nerve to do those things."

His life was altered when he met Lib Hatcher. She owned a restaurant. She hired Randy to cook, clean up, and sing for the customers. During this period, she helped him straighten out his life. One night, a talent scout from Warner Records heard Travis sing. She immediately gave him a contract. His first record was released twice. The first time, it didn't even make the top 50. The second time, it soared to number 1 on the charts.

Today Travis travels much of the year. Hatcher is his business manager and his best friend. Travis likes to perform for his fans. "They feel like family when they like you," he admits, with a shy smile. Travis still has one goal. He has received numerous awards for his singing, but he wants to be recognized as a songwriter, too. Today most of his troubles seem to be the ones expressed in his songs.

## UNDERSTANDING THE STORY

>>>> *Circle the letter next to each correct statement.*

1. The main idea of this story is that
   a. Randy Travis was a wild teenager.
   b. country music is popular.
   c. country music changed Travis's life.

2. Randy Travis knows what country songs are about because
   a. his own life has been easy and unhurried.
   b. his early life was full of trouble and pain.
   c. he was born in North Carolina.

# MAKE AN ALPHABETICAL LIST

>>>> *Here are the ten vocabulary words in this lesson. Write them in alphabetical order in the spaces below.*

| | | | | |
|---|---|---|---|---|
| urged | contract | arrested | manager | ignorance |
| recognized | altered | soared | talent | shy |

1. altered
2. arrested
3. contract
4. ignorance
5. manager

6. recognized
7. shy
8. soared
9. talent
10. urged

# WHAT DO THE WORDS MEAN?

>>>> *Following are some meanings, or definitions, for the ten vocabulary words in this lesson. Write the words next to their definitions.*

1. ignorance    a lack of knowledge
2. contract    a legal paper promising a job
3. talent    a natural gift for doing something
4. recognized    identified
5. manager    a performer's business arranger
6. arrested    held by the police
7. urged    advised strongly
8. altered    changed
9. shy    modest; uncertain
10. soared    rose upward quickly

40

# COMPLETE THE SENTENCES

>>>> *Use the vocabulary words in this lesson to complete the following sentences. Use each word only once.*

| | | | | |
|---|---|---|---|---|
| urged | contract | arrested | manager | ignorance |
| recognized | altered | soared | talent | shy |

1. Time has _____altered_____ Randy Travis's feelings about life.

2. He thinks his _____ignorance_____ got him into trouble.

3. He was _____arrested_____, but he never went to prison.

4. He has a natural _____talent_____ for singing country songs.

5. The woman who helped Travis change his life is now his _____manager_____.

6. An agent from a large record company offered Travis a _____contract_____.

7. Travis is _____shy_____ when he talks about his success as a singer.

8. He would really like to be _____recognized_____ as a songwriter.

9. He is still glad that his father _____urged_____ him to practice the guitar.

10. Travis's popularity has _____soared_____.

# USE YOUR OWN WORDS

>>>> *Look at the picture. What words come into your mind other than the ten vocabulary words used in this lesson? Write them on the blank lines below. To help you get started, here are two good words:*

1. _____cheerful_____
2. _____performer_____
3. _____Answers will vary._____
4. _____
5. _____
6. _____
7. _____
8. _____
9. _____
10. _____

# FIND THE ANTONYMS

>>>> **Antonyms** are words that are opposite in meaning. For example, *good* and *bad* and *fast* and *slow* are antonyms. Here are antonyms for six of the vocabulary words.

>>>> *See if you can find the vocabulary words and write them in the blanks on the left.*

| Vocabulary Word | Antonym |
|---|---|
| 1. _____altered_____ | unchanged |
| 2. _____shy_____ | boastful |
| 3. _____ignorance_____ | wisdom |
| 4. _____soared_____ | dropped |
| 5. _____recognized_____ | ignored |
| 6. _____urged_____ | discouraged |

# COMPLETE THE STORY

>>>> Here are the ten vocabulary words for this lesson:

| | | | | |
|---|---|---|---|---|
| urged | contract | arrested | manager | ignorance |
| recognized | altered | soared | talent | shy |

>>>> *There are six blank spaces in the story below. Four vocabulary words have already been used in the story. They are underlined. Use the other six words to fill in the blanks.*

Randy Travis is _____shy_____ in interviews. He seems surprised that people recognize him. He talks about being _____arrested_____ and about other teenage troubles. He says that his ignorance got him into trouble. Lib Hatcher _____altered_____ his life. She gave him his first job. She _____urged_____ him to sing for her customers. She recognized his _____talent_____ as a country singer. That job led to a recording contract. Hatcher is his business _____manager_____ now. His popularity soared, but Travis still thinks of himself as just a country boy.

## Learn More About Country Music

>>>> *On a separate sheet of paper or in your notebook or journal, complete one or more of the activities below.*

### Building Language

Listen to a recording of a country song. Ask a friend to help you if you cannot understand some of the language. Then write what you think the song is saying and what the singer wants to communicate.

### Learning Across the Curriculum

Country music has a long and fascinating history in this country. Read an account of how country-and-western music began. Share your information with the class.

### Broadening Your Understanding

Locate a song book with country-and-western songs. Read the lyrics. Then write a paragraph explaining what these songs are about. Are there some themes that seem to come up again and again in country-and-western music? Explain what these themes are in an oral presentation.

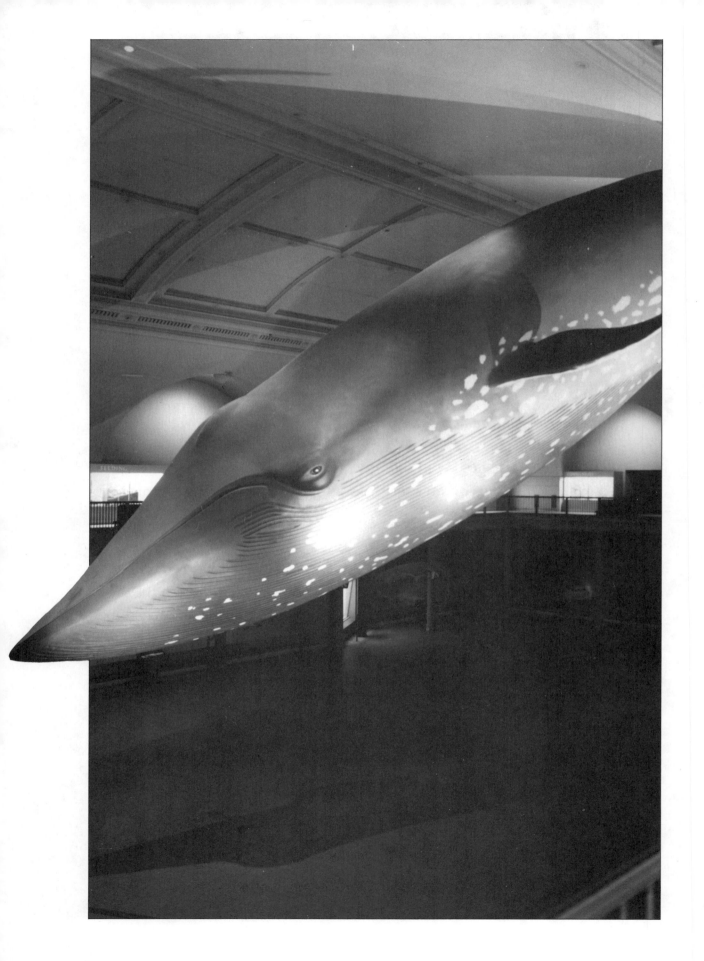

# 8 BLUE WHALES

Whales are among the largest, most powerful animals that have ever lived. Some dinosaurs were small by comparison. The blue whale, the largest of all whales, can grow to more than 100 feet and weigh 150 tons. Despite its *tremendous* size, the blue whale is *vulnerable* to hunters.

The blue whale was first hunted by the North American Inuit (Eskimos). In fact, whales were *essential* to the Inuit's existence. For centuries, they hunted these huge *mammals.* They used the whales for food, but nothing was wasted. The whale oil became fuel. The sinews became ropes. The bones were used as tools.

Today the blue whale is still hunted by some nations. Its oil is used to make soap and other products. But there are alternative sources for all of these products. People no longer need to hunt blue whales to survive.

Modern-day whalers use advanced *apparatus.* Radar and helicopters are used to find the whales. Deadly *harpoon* guns are used to kill them. The *carnage* resulting from the use of this equipment has brought the blue whale close to extinction.

*Conservationists* have warned us. If we allow whalers to continue in this way, *extermination* of the blue whale is almost certain.

It would be a shameful loss if the number of blue whales *dwindled* to nothing. The blue whale can never be replaced.

## UNDERSTANDING THE STORY

 *Circle the letter next to each correct statement.*

1. The main purpose of this story is to
   a. describe the features of the blue whale.
   b. warn readers that the blue whale is in danger of becoming extinct.
   c. describe the many ways the Inuit used whales in their daily life.

2. From this story, you can conclude that
   a. it is only a rumor that the blue whale is in danger of becoming extinct.
   b. the blue whale has learned to avoid the deadly harpoon gun.
   c. the public must do something soon if the blue whale is to survive.

# MAKE AN ALPHABETICAL LIST

>>>> *Here are the ten vocabulary words in this lesson. Write them in alphabetical order in the spaces below.*

| tremendous | extermination | mammals | essential | harpoon |
| apparatus | conservationists | carnage | dwindled | vulnerable |

1. _____apparatus_____
2. _____carnage_____
3. _____conservationists_____
4. _____dwindled_____
5. _____essential_____

6. _____extermination_____
7. _____harpoon_____
8. _____mammals_____
9. _____tremendous_____
10. _____vulnerable_____

# WHAT DO THE WORDS MEAN?

>>>> *Following are some meanings, or definitions, for the ten vocabulary words in this lesson. Write the words next to their definitions.*

1. _____tremendous_____ huge; enormous

2. _____carnage_____ the killing of a great number of people or animals

3. _____mammals_____ animals that feed milk to their young; people belong to this group

4. _____essential_____ absolutely necessary

5. _____apparatus_____ materials, tools, special instruments, or machinery needed to carry out a purpose

6. _____conservationists_____ persons who wish to save forms of animal and plant life that are in danger of being destroyed forever

7. _____harpoon_____ a long spear with a rope tied to it used in killing a whale

8. _____vulnerable_____ defenseless against; open to attack or injury

9. _____extermination_____ the act of destroying completely; putting an end to

10. _____dwindled_____ reduced in number

46

# COMPLETE THE SENTENCES

>>>> *Use the vocabulary words in this lesson to complete the following sentences. Use each word only once.*

| | | | | |
|---|---|---|---|---|
| apparatus | dwindled | harpoon | mammals | extermination |
| essential | tremendous | carnage | vulnerable | conservationists |

1. Not enough is being done to prevent the ____extermination____ of the blue whale.

2. Whales have become more ____vulnerable____ to extermination.

3. In some areas, the number of blue whales has ____dwindled____ to only a few dozen.

4. Animals that feed milk to their young are called ____mammals____.

5. The ____apparatus____ used to hunt whales today is very advanced.

6. The whale was ____essential____ to the Inuit's existence.

7. The ____carnage____ of the whale that still goes on today is harder to excuse.

8. The ____harpoon____ that used to be thrown by a person is now shot out of a gun.

9. ____Conservationists____ are calling on people to outlaw the killing of whales.

10. Blue whales are ____tremendous____ in size.

# USE YOUR OWN WORDS

>>>> *Look at the picture. What words come into your mind other than the ten vocabulary words used in this lesson? Write them on the lines below. To help you get started, here are two good words:*

1. ____water____
2. ____splash____
3. ____Answers will vary.____
4. _____
5. _____
6. _____
7. _____
8. _____
9. _____
10. _____

# MAKE POSSESSIVE WORDS

>>>> The possessive of a word shows that something belongs to it. For example, Bill has a boat; it is *Bill's* boat. To make a possessive of a word that doesn't end in *s*, add an apostrophe and an *s* to the word, such as *baker's* bread or *father's* car. To make a possessive of a word that does end in *s*, add an apostrophe (*s'*), such as *friends'* bicycles or *ladies'* hats.

>>>> *Here are ten words from the story. In the space next to the word, write the correct possessive of the word.*

1. ships _____ships'_____
2. fleet _____fleet's_____
3. ocean _____ocean's_____
4. bodies _____bodies'_____
5. whale _____whale's_____

6. Inuit _____Inuit's_____
7. whalers _____whalers'_____
8. conservationists _____conservationists'_____
9. hunter _____hunter's_____
10. boats _____boats'_____

# COMPLETE THE STORY

>>>> Here are the ten vocabulary words for this lesson:

| | | | | |
|---|---|---|---|---|
| extermination | conservationists | tremendous | essential | harpoon |
| carnage | apparatus | vulnerable | dwindled | mammals |

>>>> *There are six blank spaces in the story below. Four vocabulary words have already been used in the story. They are underlined. Use the other six words to fill in the blanks.*

The blue whale is the largest animal that has ever lived. However, _____conservationists_____ are worried. If whalers keep killing these huge _____mammals_____, the blue whale is doomed to <u>extermination</u>.

Sixty years ago, there were many blue whales in the world. Today the number has _____dwindled_____ to very few. The deadly _____harpoon_____ gun is the major reason for this. Whalers have more modern <u>apparatus</u> to help them find and kill the whales. The common use of helicopters and radar makes the whales very _____vulnerable_____.

It is <u>essential</u> that the killing of this _____tremendous_____ animal be stopped. If the <u>carnage</u> continues, the blue whale will completely disappear from the oceans of the world.

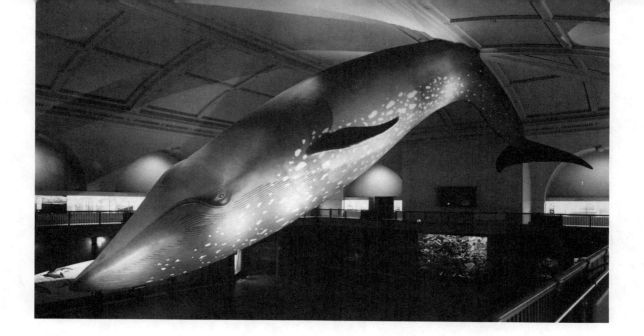

## Learn More About Endangered Species

>>>> *On a separate sheet of paper or in your notebook or journal, complete one or more of the activities below.*

### Learning Across the Curriculum

Why do animals become endangered or extinct? What can we do to stop these animals from dying out? Do some research to find out. Then write a children's book that explains the problems of endangered species and what we can do to solve this problem.

### Broadening Your Understanding

Choose an animal that has become extinct. Find out more about it and write a report on the animal. Explain what happened to it and why. If you can, include a drawing or an illustration of the animal you wrote about.

### Extending Your Reading

What is being done today to protect whales from extinction? Read one of these books to find out. Then write a paragraph that explains what you discovered, or tell one specific way in which whales are being protected.

*Saving the Whales,* by Michael Bright
*Whales and Dolphins,* by Steve Parker
*Humpback Whale,* by Michael Bright
*All About Whales,* by Deborah Kovacs

# 9 THE MARY ROSE

In 1545, the pride of the English navy, the *Mary Rose,* set sail. Its mission was to fight the French. Among those watching from shore was the monarch, Henry VIII. The crowd was cheering when the ship left Portsmouth harbor. The outcome, however, was disaster. The 700-ton *Mary Rose* was laden with cannons. Before it got far from shore, it sank. Historians say the cannons were not properly bolted. The loose cannons rolled across the deck and through the ship's side. In rushed the sea. More than 650 sailors lost their lives. It was a grave blow to the English people and their king.

More than 420 years later, the *Mary Rose* was found. A diver, Alexander McKee, discovered the wreck a mile off the coast of England. For four years, McKee and his friends worked to clear away mud and silt. They finally brought up a cannon. This find stirred the public's interest. Money was contributed to raise the *Mary Rose.* Prince Charles became president of the Mary Rose Trust, which raised funds.

The salvage continued during the summer of 1982. With the use of a special lifting crane and cradle, the *Mary Rose* was brought to the surface. Most of its oak frame was still in fair condition. To prevent further decay, the hull was wrapped in plastic sheeting. The rescue marked the end of a 17-year-long project. The cost had been $7 million, but it was worth every penny. The restored *Mary Rose* is now on permanent display in England.

## UNDERSTANDING THE STORY

>>>> *Circle the letter next to each correct statement.*

1. The main idea of this story is that
   a. it took $7 million to raise the *Mary Rose.*
   b. the *Mary Rose* sank without firing a shot at the enemy.
   c. after more than 400 years at the bottom of the sea, the *Mary Rose* was salvaged.

2. From this story, you can conclude that
   a. Prince Charles will continue to search for lost wrecks.
   b. from now on, cannons aboard ships will be more securely bolted.
   c. the British people felt great pride in the rescue of the *Mary Rose.*

# MAKE AN ALPHABETICAL LIST

>>>> *Here are the ten vocabulary words in this lesson. Write them in alphabetical order in the spaces below.*

| plastic | monarch | mission | bolted | laden |
|---------|---------|---------|--------|-------|
| cradle | restored | salvage | project | grave |

1. _____bolted_____
2. _____cradle_____
3. _____grave_____
4. _____laden_____
5. _____mission_____

6. _____monarch_____
7. _____plastic_____
8. _____project_____
9. _____restored_____
10. _____salvage_____

# WHAT DO THE WORDS MEAN?

>>>> *Following are some meanings, or definitions, for the ten vocabulary words in this lesson. Write the words next to their definitions.*

1. _____project_____ an undertaking; often a big, complicated job

2. _____monarch_____ a king or queen; an absolute ruler

3. _____cradle_____ a framework upon which a ship rests, usually during repair

4. _____bolted_____ fastened; held with metal fittings

5. _____mission_____ a special task

6. _____plastic_____ a synthetic or processed material

7. _____grave_____ serious; critical

8. _____salvage_____ the act of saving a ship or its cargo from the sea

9. _____laden_____ loaded; heavily burdened

10. _____restored_____ brought back to its original state; reconstructed

# COMPLETE THE SENTENCES

>>>> *Use the vocabulary words in this lesson to complete the following sentences. Use each word only once.*

| bolted | cradle | plastic | grave | monarch |
|--------|--------|---------|-------|---------|
| project | laden | salvage | restored | mission |

1. We knew that the _____salvage_____ was successful when we saw the ship's mast.

2. The cargo was securely _____bolted_____ to the deck so that it wouldn't roll.

3. It may take three years for the ship to be _____restored_____ to its former glory.

4. The king said, "Your _____mission_____ is to seek out and destroy the enemy."

5. Little did the _____monarch_____ know that his favorite ship would soon sink.

6. The problem was that the ship was _____laden_____ with heavy cannons.

7. The _____project_____ involved hundreds of people and millions of dollars.

8. A steel _____cradle_____ was designed to support the waterlogged ship.

9. The loss of 650 sailors was a _____grave_____ blow to the English people.

10. _____Plastic_____ was wrapped around the decaying hull to keep it from the air.

# USE YOUR OWN WORDS

>>>> *Look at the picture. What words come into your mind other than the ten vocabulary words used in this lesson? Write them on the lines below. To help you get started, here are two good words:*

1. _____mechanical_____
2. _____calm_____
3. _____Answers will vary._____
4. _____
5. _____
6. _____
7. _____
8. _____
9. _____
10. _____

# MATCH TERMS WITH THEIR MEANINGS

>>>> *Here are some words selected from the world of sailing and ships. See if you can match the terms with their meanings. You may need the help of a dictionary.*

1. **hull** _____d_____    **a.** the left-hand side of a ship

2. **port** _____a_____    **b.** a long pole holding sails

3. **starboard** _____g_____    **c.** the vertical blade at the rear of a ship, used to change course

4. **stern** _____f_____    **d.** the body of a ship

5. **mast** _____b_____    **e.** having to do with ships and the sea

6. **rudder** _____c_____    **f.** the back or rear of a ship

7. **nautical** _____e_____    **g.** the right-hand side of a ship

# COMPLETE THE STORY

>>>> Here are the ten vocabulary words for this lesson:

| | | | | |
|---|---|---|---|---|
| monarch | salvage | restored | bolted | project |
| grave | laden | plastic | cradle | mission |

>>>> *There are six blank spaces in the story below. Four vocabulary words have already been used in the story. They are underlined. Use the other six words to fill in the blanks.*

The _____monarch_____ Henry VIII was in a good mood. His fleet was on its way to fight the French. It was a <u>mission</u> that he strongly supported. He was particularly proud of the flagship, the *Mary Rose*. It was _____laden_____ with 91 cannons. What firepower!

Then suddenly everything went wrong. The heavy cannons were not _____bolted_____ well enough. They rolled across the deck and crashed through the ship's side. The ship went down. Many sailors were drowned. What a <u>grave</u> loss to the nation! But 437 years later, the *Mary Rose* was <u>restored</u> to life. A _____salvage_____ brought the *Mary Rose* to the surface. It was a huge <u>project</u> but it succeeded. A special steel _____cradle_____ was built to raise the hull. As soon as the hull reappeared, it was wrapped in _____plastic_____ to prevent further decay. The *Mary Rose* was home again.

## Learn More About Sailing Ships

>>>> *On a separate sheet of paper or in your notebook or journal, complete one or more of the activities below.*

### Learning Across the Curriculum

How did early sailors know where they were going? Ancient people who sailed the seas invented many devices to help them navigate. Among these are the kamal, the astrolabe, the sextant, the magnetic compass, and the sundial. Find out more about one of these devices. In a paragraph or two, explain how it worked. If you can, make a model of it to show to the class.

### Broadening Your Understanding

Research life on sailing ships in the 1500s. You can also look for information about life on the *Mary Rose*. Both *Time* and *Newsweek* magazines had stories about the salvage that raised the ship. Write an account of what you think life was like for the sailors on board the ship. You may want to write your account as if you were a sailor on the ship keeping a log, or diary.

### Extending Your Reading

Create a timeline of the history of sailing ships. The books below will aid your research:

*Ships, Sailors and the Sea,* by Richard Humble
*Ships Come Aboard,* by Seigfried Aust

# 10 BIGFOOT

It is the first night of your camping trip. You are sitting with your friends around the campfire. You think back to the day's activities. You were *fascinated* by all the *spectacular* sights.

Your guide interrupts your thoughts and begins to tell a chilling story. "A gigantic, wild, hairy beast that looks and walks like a man roams all over this country," the guide says. "Many *reputable* people claim to have seen it. One rancher says he has taken motion pictures of it. No one knows where this creature comes from or where it goes. No one has been able to *identify* it. The creature is called Bigfoot."

You are *skeptical* about the whole story. "It makes good *fiction,*" you think to yourself, "but it couldn't be true." Later, as you begin to fall asleep, you decide the story is nothing but a *hoax.*

Soon you are jolted awake by the shouts of one of your companions. "There it is!" You quickly look in the direction he is pointing. A huge animal, covered with dark hair, is coming toward you. But the shouts scare the *primitive* beast away.

The next morning, you think there must be an *explanation* for what happened. Was it a dream? But soon you find the *proof* you need—trampled grass and a few broken branches. No, it wasn't a dream. As you get ready for breakfast, you wonder, "Have I seen Bigfoot?"

## UNDERSTANDING THE STORY

 *Circle the letter next to each correct statement.*

1. The main purpose of this story is to
   **a.** cause the reader to wonder if Bigfoot really exists.
   **b.** show how exciting camping can be with the right people along.
   **c.** warn the reader about the dangers of camping.

2. From this story, you can conclude that
   **a.** the story of Bigfoot has finally been proved untrue.
   **b.** there will probably always be reports of seeing Bigfoot.
   **c.** Bigfoot is really a huge bear.

# MAKE AN ALPHABETICAL LIST

>>>> *Here are the ten vocabulary words in this lesson. Write them in alphabetical order in the spaces below.*

| fascinated | spectacular | reputable | identify | skeptical |
|---|---|---|---|---|
| fiction | hoax | primitive | explanation | proof |

1. explanation
2. fascinated
3. fiction
4. hoax
5. identify

6. primitive
7. proof
8. reputable
9. skeptical
10. spectacular

# WHAT DO THE WORDS MEAN?

>>>> *Following are some meanings, or definitions, for the ten vocabulary words in this lesson. Write the words next to their definitions.*

1. skeptical — having doubts; not willing to believe
2. hoax — a trick
3. identify — to recognize as being a particular person or thing
4. fascinated — amazed; very interested by
5. fiction — a story that is not true
6. proof — facts; evidence
7. reputable — honorable; well thought of
8. spectacular — eye-catching; very unusual
9. primitive — living long ago; from earliest times
10. explanation — a statement that clears up a difficulty or a mistake

# COMPLETE THE SENTENCES

>>>> *Use the vocabulary words in this lesson to complete the following sentences. Use each word only once.*

| | | | | |
|---|---|---|---|---|
| fiction | spectacular | skeptical | hoax | proof |
| primitive | explanation | identify | fascinated | reputable |

1. People have always been ____fascinated____ by stories of strange creatures.

2. The story of Bigfoot seems closer to science ____fiction____ than to fact.

3. A professor called the Bigfoot story a ____hoax____.

4. She said that she needed more ____proof____, such as a clear photograph.

5. Her ____explanation____ of broken branches wasn't convincing.

6. She wasn't able to ____identify____ a piece of hair found clinging to a branch.

7. Those who claim to have seen Bigfoot seem ____reputable____.

8. The camper saw many ____spectacular____ sights that day.

9. The police were ____skeptical____ when two people in different places reported seeing Bigfoot at the same time.

10. The monster is called ____primitive____ because it seems like something prehistoric.

# USE YOUR OWN WORDS

>>>> *Look at the picture. What words come into your mind other than the ten vocabulary words used in this lesson? Write them on the lines below. To help you get started, here are two good words:*

1. ____leaves____
2. ____hairy____
3. ____Answers will vary.____
4. _____
5. _____
6. _____
7. _____
8. _____
9. _____
10. _____

# MAKE NEW WORDS FROM OLD

>>>> *Look at the vocabulary word below. See how many words you can form by using the letters of this word. Make up at least ten words. One has already been done for you. Write your words in the spaces below.*

Answers may vary.

## reputable

1. _____plate_____
2. _____table_____
3. _____able_____
4. _____put_____
5. _____pub_____
6. _____tear_____

7. _____bear_____
8. _____bare_____
9. _____art_____
10. _____tab_____
11. _____bat_____
12. _____bleat_____

# COMPLETE THE STORY

>>>> Here are the ten vocabulary words for this lesson:

| | | | | |
|---|---|---|---|---|
| fascinated | spectacular | reputable | identify | skeptical |
| fiction | hoax | primitive | explanation | proof |

>>>> *There are six blank spaces in the story below. Four vocabulary words have already been used in the story. They are underlined. Use the other six words to fill in the blanks.*

Many _____reputable_____ people claim they have seen Bigfoot, although scientists are _____skeptical_____ about this beast. Some experts think Bigfoot is nothing but a hoax.

One thing is sure: Huge footprints have been found in the areas where the primitive creature roams. No one has been able to _____identify_____ these spectacular tracks. No one has ever seen anything like them before.

Bigfoot has _____fascinated_____ many people. Some believe Bigfoot is real; others say it is just _____fiction_____. Scientists hope to gather more _____proof_____ about Bigfoot. Then, hopefully, we will have an explanation about this strange and mysterious creature.

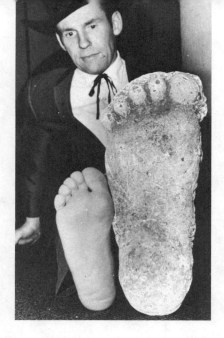

## Learn More About Monsters

>>>> *On a separate sheet of paper or in your notebook or journal, complete one or more of the activities below.*

### Appreciating Diversity

Monsters, real or imaginary, are a part of many cultures. Think back to your childhood and remember the frightening stories you were told. Write one down. How is it like the Bigfoot story? How is it different?

### Broadening Your Understanding

Find out more about Bigfoot. Research this creature. Write a report arguing that Bigfoot either does or does not exist. Find a friend with the opposite opinion. Have a debate with your friend about the existence of Bigfoot. Have the class vote on whose argument is more convincing.

### Extending Your Reading

Read one of the books below about movie monsters. Then watch a movie about a monster, such as Godzilla. Finally, write a paragraph that explains why people think the monster is frightening.

*Horror in the Movies,* by Daniel Cohen
*Frankenstein,* by John Turvey
*Movie Monsters,* by Thomas G. Aylesworth
*Dracula,* by Ian Thorne

# 11 THE LEARNING MAN

Gordon Parks is a $\boxed{notable}$ photographer. People love his pictures because he uses his camera the way a painter uses a brush.

Parks learned about photography at a Chicago art center. He became $\boxed{enthusiastic}$ about the idea of $\boxed{pursuing}$ a career in this field. To earn money, he worked as a waiter, a lumberjack, and a piano player. He led a band. He even played baseball.

Everyone saw that Parks's talent was $\boxed{considerable.}$ He won a $\boxed{scholarship.}$ Now he had an opportunity to study without worrying about money.

In time, Parks became a top magazine photographer. He traveled all over the world, creating wonderful stories in pictures. Among his $\boxed{assignments}$ were stories on $\boxed{segregation}$ and crime. He also wrote a report on the life of a gang leader in New York's Harlem. He also made a $\boxed{documentary}$ of his story on the $\boxed{plight}$ of a poor boy in Brazil.

The accomplishments of this man are many. Parks is known for his original music. He is a master of the documentary. His novel *The Learning Tree* is based on his life. It was made into a movie that Parks produced, directed, and photographed. In 1989, *The Learning Tree* was declared one of the national treasures of American film.

Gordon Parks has found time for not one $\boxed{profession}$ but three—photography, music, and writing—and has reached the top in all three.

## UNDERSTANDING THE STORY

 *Circle the letter next to each correct statement.*

1. The main idea of this story is that
   a. Parks won a scholarship that allowed him to study photography.
   b. Parks is a master of the documentary.
   c. Parks is a person of many accomplishments.

2. From this story, you can conclude that
   a. Parks's wide experience is helpful to him in his work.
   b. Parks will win an Academy Award for one of his documentaries.
   c. Parks is ruining his health by trying to do too much.

# MAKE AN ALPHABETICAL LIST

>>>> *Here are the ten vocabulary words in this lesson. Write them in alphabetical order in the spaces below.*

| | | | | |
|---|---|---|---|---|
| notable | pursuing | enthusiastic | profession | scholarship |
| considerable | documentary | segregation | assignments | plight |

1. _____ assignments _____
2. _____ considerable _____
3. _____ documentary _____
4. _____ enthusiastic _____
5. _____ notable _____

6. _____ plight _____
7. _____ profession _____
8. _____ pursuing _____
9. _____ scholarship _____
10. _____ segregation _____

# WHAT DO THE WORDS MEAN?

>>>> *Following are some meanings, or definitions, for the ten vocabulary words in this lesson. Write the words next to their definitions.*

1. _____ profession _____ an occupation requiring an education

2. _____ pursuing _____ striving for

3. _____ scholarship _____ money given to help a student pay for studies

4. _____ assignments _____ definite tasks or jobs to be done; specific works to be accomplished

5. _____ enthusiastic _____ eagerly interested

6. _____ documentary _____ a factual presentation of a scene, place, or condition of life in writing or on film

7. _____ plight _____ a condition or state, usually bad

8. _____ notable _____ worthy of notice; remarkable

9. _____ considerable _____ not a little; much

10. _____ segregation _____ separation from others; setting individuals or groups apart from society

# COMPLETE THE SENTENCES

>>>> *Use the vocabulary words in this lesson to complete the following sentences. Use each word only once.*

| | | | | |
|---|---|---|---|---|
| scholarship | pursuing | considerable | profession | assignments |
| enthusiastic | plight | segregation | notable | documentary |

1. The ___documentary___ *The Learning Tree* is based on Gordon Parks's life.

2. To succeed in one ___profession___ is good, but to succeed in three is exceptional.

3. You are happy to accept all sorts of ___assignments___ if you are a young photographer just breaking into the field.

4. Among Parks's ___notable___ achievements is a documentary about a boy in Brazil.

5. The ___plight___ of the poor has always interested Parks.

6. The critics were most ___enthusiastic___ in their reviews of Parks's latest film.

7. If he had not received a ___scholarship___, he could not have finished school.

8. As director, he spent ___considerable___ time interviewing actors before picking a lead.

9. Parks made people more aware of the problem of ___segregation___.

10. Parks is a person who believes in ___pursuing___ his interests.

# USE YOUR OWN WORDS

>>>> *Look at the picture. What words come into your mind other than the ten vocabulary words used in this lesson? Write them on the lines below. To help you get started, here are two good words:*

1. ___moustache___
2. ___camera___
3. ___Answers will vary.___
4. _____
5. _____
6. _____
7. _____
8. _____
9. _____
10. _____

# FIND THE SUBJECTS AND PREDICATES

>>>> The **subject** of a sentence names the person, place, or thing that is spoken about. The **predicate** of a sentence is what is said about the subject. For example:

The small boy went to the football game.

>>>> *The small boy* is the subject (the person the sentence is talking about). *Went to the football game* is the predicate of the sentence (because it tells what the small boy did).

>>>> *In the following sentences, draw one line under the subject of the sentence and two lines under the predicate of the sentence.*

1. I hungered for learning.

2. A scholarship allowed me to finish my education.

3. Two assignments impressed me.

4. The other was a documentary that I wrote.

5. My most notable achievement was writing the book.

# COMPLETE THE STORY

>>>> Here are the ten vocabulary words for this lesson:

| | | | | |
|---|---|---|---|---|
| considerable | profession | assignments | scholarship | enthusiastic |
| documentary | notable | plight | pursuing | segregation |

>>>> *There are six blank spaces in the story below. Four vocabulary words have already been used in the story. They are underlined. Use the other six words to fill in the blanks.*

Gordon Parks has had considerable success in not one _____profession_____ but three. However, his most _____notable_____ assignments have been on one subject—people.

Parks's _____enthusiastic_____ love of humanity is shown in many of the picture stories he has photographed over the years. One particular documentary about a Brazilian boy shows what it is like to be poor.

His novel *The Learning Tree*, which is based on his own life, shows the _____plight_____ of people who must live under segregation.

It all started for Parks when he was awarded a _____scholarship_____ many years ago. Since then, he has been _____pursuing_____ one special goal—to show how people live. Hopefully, his work will teach us to understand each other better too.

## Learn More About Photography

>>>> *On a separate sheet of paper or in your notebook or journal, complete one or more of the activities below.*

### Building Language

In a magazine, find a photograph that moves you. If you can, describe the photograph in a language other than English. Write the words in your native language that describe it. Now use English to describe the same picture. How are your descriptions the same or different?

### Learning Across the Curriculum

Matthew Brady was one of the first important American photographers. Find out something about Matthew Brady. Look at his photographs of the Civil War. Now find some drawings that illustrate the Revolutionary War. How can looking at photographs change what people think about a war?

### Broadening Your Understanding

Cut out photographs and captions from the news section of a newspaper. Then look critically at the photographs. Which photographs do you think work the best? Why? Which photographs do not impress you? What do you think is the most important quality for a news photograph to have? Write a paragraph expressing your ideas.

# 12 RICH AND AMOS

Horatio Alger, a famous writer of the last century, wrote about rags-to-riches heroes. His characters always became $\boxed{\textbf{\textit{prosperous}}}$ by honest and hard work. So it seems $\boxed{\textbf{\textit{appropriate}}}$ that Wally Amos should be one of the winners of the Horatio Alger Association awards.

Amos is a real Horatio Alger hero. As a young man in Tallahassee, Florida, he was so poor that he had to walk 6 miles to learn a $\boxed{\textbf{\textit{trade.}}}$ He couldn't afford the bus $\boxed{\textbf{\textit{fare.}}}$

Then Amos started his own business and sold about $12 million worth of his Famous Amos cookies every year. He was the first to open stores that sold only his cookies. You could buy his $\boxed{\textbf{\textit{products}}}$ all over the United States and even in Asia. Wally Amos sold his business in 1985. He now lives in Hawaii and has a new cookie business. He is $\boxed{\textbf{\textit{definitely}}}$ a rags-to-riches hero!

It isn't all hard work, though. Amos is active in $\boxed{\textbf{\textit{literacy}}}$ programs. He strongly supports $\boxed{\textbf{\textit{efforts}}}$ to teach people to read and write. He also wants people to enjoy themselves. "It's okay to have fun while doing important work," he says. He proved his point during a recent meeting to promote literacy by playing "California, Here I Come" on a kazoo.

Perhaps the secret of his success is that Amos enjoys his job. $\boxed{\textbf{\textit{Authorities}}}$ say that successful people like what they do. Amos certainly likes what he does, and so do lots of other people. Amos received one of the first presidential awards for new business excellence from a famous $\boxed{\textbf{\textit{fan,}}}$ Ronald Reagan.

## UNDERSTANDING THE STORY

 *Circle the letter next to each correct statement.*

1. The main purpose of this story is to
   a. tell how to make chocolate chip cookies.
   **b.** tell about a successful and hard-working man.
   c. explain how to win awards for hard work.

2. From this story, you can conclude that
   a. Amos did not like a regular job.
   b. chocolate chip cookies are easy to make.
   **c.** people liked Amos's chocolate chip cookies.

# MAKE AN ALPHABETICAL LIST

>>>> *Here are the ten vocabulary words in this lesson. Write them in alphabetical order in the spaces below.*

| prosperous | definitely | appropriate | literacy | trade |
|---|---|---|---|---|
| efforts | fare | authorities | products | fan |

1. appropriate
2. authorities
3. definitely
4. efforts
5. fan

6. fare
7. literacy
8. products
9. prosperous
10. trade

# WHAT DO THE WORDS MEAN?

>>>> *Following are some meanings, or definitions, for the ten vocabulary words in this lesson. Write the words next to their definitions.*

1. efforts — attempts
2. appropriate — proper
3. trade — a job; a skill
4. definitely — absolutely
5. products — manufactured items
6. authorities — specialists
7. fare — the cost of a ticket
8. fan — an enthusiastic supporter
9. literacy — the ability to read and write
10. prosperous — successful

# COMPLETE THE SENTENCES

>>>> *Use the vocabulary words in this lesson to complete the following sentences. Use each word only once.*

| prosperous | definitely | appropriate | literacy | trade |
|---|---|---|---|---|
| efforts | fare | authorities | products | fan |

1. Wally Amos _____definitely_____ had a better idea for cookies.

2. He was too poor to pay his bus _____fare_____ as a young man.

3. He learned a _____trade_____ in Tallahassee, but it wasn't baking cookies.

4. Through his own _____efforts_____, Amos became a wealthy businessman.

5. His baked _____products_____ are sold in the United States and Asia.

6. Amos believes that you can have fun even as you become _____prosperous_____.

7. It seems _____appropriate_____ that Amos should tell other people to learn how to have fun.

8. Many _____authorities_____ have studied how Amos became a success.

9. Amos also gives time to _____literacy_____ programs.

10. He can even count a President of the United States as a _____fan_____.

# USE YOUR OWN WORDS

>>>> *Look at the picture. What words come into your mind other than the ten vocabulary words used in this lesson? Write them on the lines below. To help you get started, here are two good words:*

1. _____smiles_____
2. _____hats_____
3. ___Answers will vary.___
4. _____
5. _____
6. _____
7. _____
8. _____
9. _____
10. _____

# MAKE POSSESSIVE WORDS

>>>> The possessive of a word shows that something belongs to it. For example, Wally has a plan; it is *Wally's* plan. To make a possessive of a word that doesn't end in *s*, add an apostrophe and an *s* to the word, such as *cookie's* price or *store's* shelf. To make a possessive of a word that does end in *s*, add an apostrophe (') after the *s*, such as *cookies'* chips or *stores'* sales. (A proper name ending in *s* is an exception: *Amos's* cookies.)

>>>> *Here are ten words from the story. In the blank space next to each word, write the correct possessive of each word.*

1. Alger ___Alger's___          6. United States ___United States'___

2. heroes ___heroes'___          7. awards ___awards'___

3. people ___people's___          8. Reagan ___Reagan's___

4. meeting ___meeting's___          9. winners ___winners'___

5. kazoo ___kazoo's___          10. rags ___rags'___

# COMPLETE THE STORY

>>>> Here are the ten vocabulary words for this lesson:

| | | | | |
|---|---|---|---|---|
| prosperous | definitely | appropriate | literacy | trade |
| efforts | fare | authorities | products | fan |

>>>> *There are six blank spaces in the story below. Four vocabulary words have already been used in the story. They are underlined. Use the other six words to fill in the blanks.*

A ___prosperous___ businessperson must be ready for hard work. The main idea is to sell the ___products___ of the business. Success takes great <u>efforts</u> each day. It is ___definitely___ not easy. You may become discouraged as you give your bus ___fare___ to the driver again and again every day. Yet you should never give up hope!

There are some things you can do to prepare for success. Reading and writing are important, so work on your ___literacy___ skills. The <u>authorities</u> who study business success also say you must be prepared to do things yourself. That is ___appropriate___ after all, if you want to know how your business works. You can go to <u>trade</u> school to learn some useful business techniques. Read letters from your <u>fans</u>. They will tell you what to change and what to leave alone.

## Learn More About Business

>>>> *On a separate sheet of paper or in your notebook or journal, complete one or more of the activities below.*

### Working Together

Imagine your group is going to start a business. Decide what your business will be. Now write a business plan for your business. Have people research how much your product will cost to produce and market, how much you think you can sell it for, how many you think you can sell, and what you think your profits will be. Have someone plan an advertising campaign. Someone else can design the packaging and plan where to sell your product. Put your plans together and present them to the class.

### Broadening Your Understanding

You are in charge of creating an advertising campaign to sell Wally Amos's cookies. Think about the product and how you can interest people in it. Think of how you can show that Famous Amos cookies are better than other chocolate chip cookies. Think of who you want to buy these cookies. Now write a newspaper or magazine ad that will sell Famous Amos cookies.

### Learning Across the Curriculum

What kind of business intrigues you? Research a business you are interested in. Find out what the people do in that business. Write a summary of what you found out and whether you still think you would like to be involved in that business.

Oprah Winfrey, the popular actress and talk-show host, *embodies* an important message. That message is this: You can be born poor, black, and female and make it to the top.

Winfrey spent her first six years with her grandmother, who she says could "whip me for days and never get tired." Winfrey says her mother worked hard and wanted the best for her but did not know how to achieve these aims.

As a teenager, Winfrey rebelled and got into trouble. She went to Tennessee to live with her father, a strict *disciplinarian* who encouraged her to read a book every week. Years later, in 1971, Oprah became Miss Black Tennessee. In 1976, she joined the ABC *affiliate* WJZ-TV in Baltimore as conewsperson. But it was her film acting that brought her national fame. Winfrey won an Academy Award nomination for her role as Sophia in the film of Alice Walker's novel *The Color Purple*. "Luck," says Winfrey, "is a *matter* of preparation. I've been *blessed* —but I create the blessings."

Today Oprah Winfrey's name is *synonymous* with daytime talk shows. She has won six Emmys for best talk-show host. She deals with important social issues on her show. Many people think of her as an *activist.* She is concerned about *racial* problems in America. Each week, millions of Americans eagerly *await* her shows to hear about the *issues* she presents.

## UNDERSTANDING THE STORY

>>>> *Circle the letter next to each correct statement.*

1. The main idea of this story is that
   a. Oprah Winfrey was nominated for an Academy Award.
   b. despite a poor start in life, Winfrey has become very accomplished.
   c. Oprah Winfrey is upset by racial inequality.

2. From the story, you can conclude that
   a. people can overcome difficulties to accomplish what they want.
   b. Winfrey will start a new career in South Africa.
   c. Winfrey was unsuccessful as an actress.

# MAKE AN ALPHABETICAL LIST

>>>> *Here are the ten vocabulary words in this lesson. Write them in alphabetical order in the spaces below.*

| | | | | |
|---|---|---|---|---|
| issues | embodies | affiliate | matter | await |
| blessed | racial | synonymous | activist | disciplinarian |

1. activist
2. affiliate
3. await
4. blessed
5. disciplinarian

6. embodies
7. issues
8. matter
9. racial
10. synonymous

# WHAT DO THE WORDS MEAN?

>>>> *Following are some meanings, or definitions, for the ten vocabulary words in this lesson. Write the words next to their definitions.*

1. synonymous — alike in meaning or significance

2. disciplinarian — a person who believes in strict training

3. activist — a person who publicly supports a cause

4. affiliate — a person or an organization usually connected to a larger organization

5. matter — a real thing; content rather than manner or style

6. racial — of or having to do with race or origins

7. issues — topics or problems under discussion

8. blessed — given great happiness

9. await — to wait for; to expect

10. embodies — represents in real or definite form

# COMPLETE THE SENTENCES

>>>> *Use the vocabulary words in this lesson to complete the following sentences. Use each word only once.*

| | | | | |
|---|---|---|---|---|
| issues | embodies | affiliate | matter | await |
| blessed | racial | synonymous | activist | disciplinarian |

1. Winfrey has become an _____activist_____ for important causes.

2. Her program focuses on important _____issues_____ of the day.

3. Winfrey really _____embodies_____ a rags-to-riches story.

4. Winfrey's father was a _____disciplinarian_____ who encouraged education.

5. The TV station Winfrey worked for was an _____affiliate_____ of a larger station.

6. Winfrey admits that much of her success is a _____matter_____ of preparation.

7. Winfrey is very aware of the _____racial_____ problems in our society.

8. For many viewers, the name Oprah Winfrey is _____synonymous_____ with television talk shows.

9. Winfrey says she is _____blessed_____ because she helps bring about her luck.

10. Winfrey's fans _____await_____ her show every day to see who her guests will be.

# USE YOUR OWN WORDS

>>>> *Look at the picture. What words come into your mind other than the ten vocabulary words used in this lesson? Write them on the lines below. To help you get started, here are two good words:*

1. _____happy_____
2. _____smiling_____
3. ___Answers will vary.___
4. _____
5. _____
6. _____
7. _____
8. _____
9. _____
10. _____

## DO THE CROSSWORD PUZZLE

>>>> ***In a crossword puzzle, there is a group of boxes, some with numbers in them. There are also two columns of words, or definitions, one for "across" and the other for "down." Do the puzzle. Each of the words in the puzzle will be one of the vocabulary words in this lesson.***

**Across**

**3.** having to do with race

**5.** strict person

**9.** public supporter of causes

**10.** problems

**Down**

**1.** a real thing; content

**2.** makes real

**4.** to have great happiness

**6.** alike in meaning

**7.** member

**8.** to look forward to

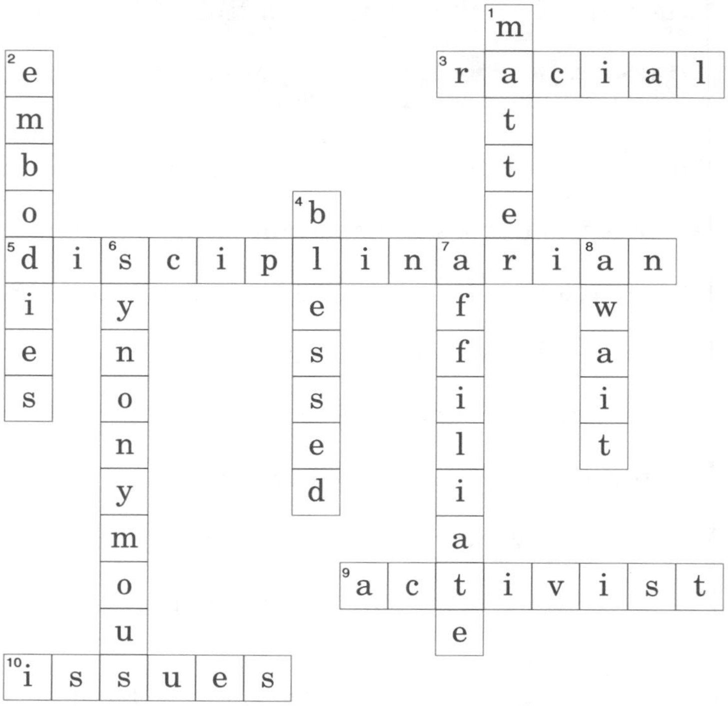

## COMPLETE THE STORY

>>>> Here are the ten vocabulary words for this lesson:

| | | | | |
|---|---|---|---|---|
| issue | embodies | affiliate | matter | await |
| blessed | racial | synonymous | activist | disciplinarian |

>>>> ***There are six blank spaces in the story below. Four vocabulary words have already been used in the story. They are underlined. Use the other six words to fill in the blanks.***

Oprah Winfrey is a successful TV talk-show host. She started working at an ABC affiliate station in Baltimore. Winfrey considers herself ____blessed____, but she knows that much of her luck has been a ____matter____ of work. She has become an activist. Every show focuses on an important social issue. For example, she is very aware of racial discrimination. Although her father was a ____disciplinarian____, Winfrey had a difficult childhood. Through work and determination, her name has become ____synonymous____ with daytime TV. Winfrey ____embodies____ the American idea that, people can succeed against great odds. Her fans ____await____ her next achievement.

## Learn More About Talk Shows

>>>> *On a separate sheet of paper or in your notebook or journal, complete one or more of the activities below.*

### Building Language

Watch a talk show on television. List the words and phrases you do not understand. Either look up the words and phrases or ask a friend what each one means. Use each word or phrase in a sentence.

### Broadening Your Understanding

Imagine you are in charge of finding topics and guests for Oprah Winfrey's talk show. Plan a week's worth of topics and the guests you would want for each one. Then explain why you chose what you did.

### Extending Your Reading

Read one of these books about television. Then plan your own talk show. What staff will you need to help put the show on the air? Consider everything from the people who plan the show to the people who help produce the show.

*Careers in Television,* by Howard Blumenthal
*Series TV,* by Malka Drucker and Elizabeth James
*Make Your Own . . .Videos, Commercials, Radio Shows,* by the Fun Group

# 14 FREEDOM FIGHTER

The stage was bare except for a piano, a bench, and one empty chair. Although the audience sat quietly, a feeling of excitement filled the room. Something great was about to happen.

The houselights dimmed. A short, stout, bald man, carrying a **cello** and a bow in one hand, walked slowly to the chair. He turned and faced the audience. The theater erupted with cheers and wild applause. Pablo Casals, the world's greatest cellist, was about to bring the room alive with his music.

Born in Spain, Casals became a freedom fighter during the Spanish civil war. But when this revolution was over, General Franco had won control over the Spanish people. He formed a **dictatorship** that **restricted** the freedom of all the Spanish people. Those who disagreed with him were shot, put in prison, or **banished** from their homeland. Casals became a sworn enemy of this **tyranny.**

Casals left his native land in **protest** against Franco's government. But he continued to fight for freedom. He **devoted** his life to helping the people of Spain. Casals organized benefit concerts in France and Puerto Rico. These music **festivals** raised money to help Spanish exiles. Casals was **motivated** by his love of freedom.

Casals played from his heart. The music from his stringed instrument was **flawless**—smooth and moving. When he died in Puerto Rico at the age of 96, Casals left behind an example for all freedom-loving people of the world.

## UNDERSTANDING THE STORY

 *Circle the letter next to each correct statement.*

1. Another good title for this story might be:
   a. "The World's Greatest Musician."
   b. "The Dangers of Dictatorship."
   c. "An Artist Against Tyranny."

2. From this story, you can conclude that
   a. people should not mix art with politics.
   b. Pablo Casals took as much pride in his political beliefs as in his music.
   c. Pablo Casals gave up his music to fight for freedom.

# MAKE AN ALPHABETICAL LIST

>>>> *Here are the ten vocabulary words in this lesson. Write them in alphabetical order in the spaces below.*

| cello | festivals | restricted | motivated | protest |
| devoted | dictatorship | tyranny | banished | flawless |

1. banished
2. cello
3. devoted
4. dictatorship
5. festivals

6. flawless
7. motivated
8. protest
9. restricted
10. tyranny

# WHAT DO THE WORDS MEAN?

>>>> *Following are some meanings, or definitions, for the ten vocabulary words in this lesson. Write the words next to their definitions.*

1. motivated — stimulated to do something; inspired

2. cello — a musical instrument similar to a violin, but much larger, that is played in a sitting position

3. restricted — limited in freedom or use

4. festivals — celebrations

5. dictatorship — the rule by one person or group that must be obeyed; power held by a few through force

6. protest — strong objection; opposition

7. flawless — perfect; without fault

8. banished — forced to leave one's country

9. devoted — gave up one's time, money, or efforts for some cause or person

10. tyranny — the cruel use of power

82

# COMPLETE THE SENTENCES

>>>> *Use the vocabulary words in this lesson to complete the following sentences. Use each word only once.*

| | | | | |
|---|---|---|---|---|
| devoted | cello | protest | tyranny | flawless |
| dictatorship | banished | motivated | festivals | restricted |

1. In _____protest_____ against the government of Franco, Pablo Casals left Spain.

2. Casals continued to fight against _____dictatorship_____.

3. When freedom of speech is _____restricted_____, it is difficult for people to express their true feelings.

4. Those who protest are often _____banished_____ from their homeland.

5. The _____tyranny_____ of a dictator causes some people to want to leave.

6. Casals _____devoted_____ most of his time to organizing benefit concerts.

7. The music _____festivals_____ he organized were successful.

8. When people talk about masters of the _____cello_____, Pablo Casals is the name most often mentioned.

9. Casals was _____motivated_____ by his deep love of music to be a great cellist.

10. His playing was described as _____flawless_____ and inspiring.

# USE YOUR OWN WORDS

>>>> *Look at the picture. What words come into your mind other than the ten vocabulary words used in this lesson? Write them on the lines below. To help you get started, here are two good words:*

1. _____bow_____
2. _____strings_____
3. _____Answers will vary._____
4. _____
5. _____
6. _____
7. _____
8. _____
9. _____
10. _____

# MATCH TERMS WITH THEIR MEANINGS

>>>> *Here are some words selected from the field of music. See if you can match the terms with their meanings.*

1. **symphony** _____b_____       a. the speed at which music is played.

2. **viola** _____d_____       b. a long musical work for an orchestra

3. **tempo** _____a_____       c. when music gradually becomes louder

4. **tympanist** _____e_____       d. a member of the violin family that is between the violin and cello in size

5. **crescendo** _____c_____       e. the orchestra member who plays the kettledrums

# COMPLETE THE STORY

>>>> Here are the ten vocabulary words for this lesson:

| | | | | |
|---|---|---|---|---|
| devoted | restricted | dictatorship | cello | motivated |
| festivals | banished | tyranny | flawless | protest |

>>>> *There are six blank spaces in the story below. Four vocabulary words have already been used in the story. They are underlined. Use the other six words to fill in the blanks.*

Pablo Casals, the great _____cello_____ master, left his native Spain in _____protest_____ against General Franco's <u>dictatorship.</u>

Casals was <u>devoted</u> to peace and to helping the people of Spain. He organized music _____festivals_____ to raise money for those Spaniards who had been _____banished_____ from their homeland. In so doing, he <u>motivated</u> other people to demonstrate against _____tyranny_____.

Through his _____flawless_____ music, Casals took a courageous stand against any government that <u>restricted</u> the freedom of its citizens.

## Learn More About Music

>>>> *On a separate sheet of paper or in your notebook or journal, complete one or more of the activities below.*

### Learning Across the Curriculum

Music can stir people to action. Look in books about folk songs to find a song that was popular during a war or another time of stress for the United States. Listen to a recording of the song, if possible. Read the words. Then describe what effect you think the song might have had on people's opinions.

### Broadening Your Understanding

Find out more about the Spanish civil war in which Pablo Casals was involved. What did a freedom fighter do during the Spanish civil war? When was this revolution? What was the result of this war? In what way do you think being a freedom fighter may have influenced the way Casals performed his music?

### Extending Your Reading

Casals organized benefit concerts to help raise money for Spanish exiles. In this country, musicians have held concerts to benefit various causes. Read one of the books below about the Live Aid concerts. Then plan your own benefit concert. What cause would you benefit? What musicians would you hope to get involved?

*Live Aid,* by Susan Clinton
*Bob Geldof: The Pop Star Who Raised $170 Million for Famine Relief in Ethiopia,* by Vallance D'Ar Adrian

# 15 MOUNTAIN OF FIRE

Our bus wound its way slowly up the steep Italian mountainside through olive groves, fruit orchards, and thick forests. At 6,500 feet, we reached the end of the road. From this point on, we traveled by cable car.

The view below us was unusually beautiful. As far as we could see, the mountain was covered with sand, hardened $\boxed{lava,}$ and ashes. When we reached the end of the cable-car run, we climbed out. It was cold, but we would have to walk the rest of the way.

Our guide said, "This is a very dangerous climb. If anyone falls from the top, he or she will $\boxed{vanish}$ forever. Therefore, I must $\boxed{enforce}$ safety rules."

He went on. "An active $\boxed{volcano}$ is a weak place in the earth's crust. Extremely hot gases $\boxed{exert}$ tremendous pressure, force their way to the top, and escape from the earth's $\boxed{interior.}$ It can $\boxed{erupt}$ at any time, sending rivers of molten lava down the mountainside. A few years ago, the village of Santa d'Alfio was destroyed during an eruption. But the brave people rebuilt their town."

We carefully made our way farther up the mountain. When we reached the top, we $\boxed{gingerly}$ stepped to the edge of the fiery crater, where ropes kept us from getting too close. Clouds of smoke, steam, and black dust rose into the air, causing our eyes to $\boxed{smart.}$ Breathing was difficult. We had reached the $\boxed{peak}$ of Europe's most active volcano—Mount Etna.

## UNDERSTANDING THE STORY

>>>> *Circle the letter next to each correct statement.*

1. The main purpose of this story is to
   a. tell about the violent history of Mount Etna.
   b. tell us never to go near a volcano.
   c. describe the adventure of a group of people climbing a volcano.

2. If a volcano is said to be active, you can assume that
   a. no one is living in the area around it.
   b. it can erupt at any time.
   c. it will have a major eruption in the next month.

# MAKE AN ALPHABETICAL LIST

>>>> *Here are the ten vocabulary words in this lesson. Write them in alphabetical order in the spaces below.*

| enforce | lava | peak | exert | interior |
|---------|---------|--------|-------|----------|
| smart | gingerly | vanish | erupt | volcano |

1. _____enforce_____
2. _____erupt_____
3. _____exert_____
4. _____gingerly_____
5. _____interior_____

6. _____lava_____
7. _____peak_____
8. _____smart_____
9. _____vanish_____
10. _____volcano_____

# WHAT DO THE WORDS MEAN?

>>>> *Following are some meanings, or definitions, for the ten vocabulary words in this lesson. Write the words next to their definitions.*

1. _____smart_____ to feel a sharp pain; to sting

2. _____vanish_____ to disappear

3. _____enforce_____ to make someone do something; to compel

4. _____erupt_____ to explode; to burst forth

5. _____interior_____ inside; inner part

6. _____lava_____ melted rock that comes from a volcano

7. _____peak_____ the top; the highest point

8. _____exert_____ to apply; to use fully

9. _____gingerly_____ very carefully

10. _____volcano_____ a mountain with a cuplike crater that throws out hot melted rock and steam

# COMPLETE THE SENTENCES

>>>> *Use the vocabulary words in this lesson to complete the following sentences. Use each word only once.*

| | | | | |
|---|---|---|---|---|
| smart | erupt | interior | exert | lava |
| peak | enforce | vanish | volcano | gingerly |

1. Our eyes began to _____smart_____ from the Volcano's smoke.

2. The guide said that an active volcano may _____erupt_____ at any time.

3. We stepped _____gingerly_____ over the broken pieces of rock.

4. After a long uphill climb, we finally reached the _____peak_____ of the volcano.

5. Volcanoes result when forces beneath the earth's surface _____exert_____ pressure.

6. Mount Etna is considered to be the most active _____volcano_____ in Europe.

7. We wanted to peer into the _____interior_____ of the volcano.

8. Police _____enforce_____ laws that prohibit people from getting close to the volcano.

9. The _____lava_____ streaming down the mountainside looked like a river of fire.

10. Whole villages have been known to _____vanish_____ from sight after an eruption.

# USE YOUR OWN WORDS

>>>> *Look at the picture. What words come into your mind other than the ten vocabulary words used in this lesson? Write them on the lines below. To help you get started, here are two good words:*

1. _____smoke_____
2. _____mountain_____
3. __Answers will vary.__
4. _____
5. _____
6. _____
7. _____
8. _____
9. _____
10. _____

# IDENTIFY THE SYNONYMS AND ANTONYMS

>>>> A **synonym** is a word that means the same, or nearly the same, as another word. An **antonym** is a word that means the opposite of another word.

>>>> *There are six vocabulary words listed below. To the right of each is either a synonym or an antonym. On the line beside each pair of words, write S for synonyms or A for antonyms.*

| | | | | |
|---|---|---|---|---|
| 1. | **vanish** | appear | 1. | A |
| 2. | **peak** | bottom | 2. | A |
| 3. | **smart** | sting | 3. | S |
| 4. | **gingerly** | carelessly | 4. | A |
| 5. | **interior** | exterior | 5. | A |
| 6. | **erupt** | gush | 6. | S |

# COMPLETE THE STORY

>>>> Here are the ten vocabulary words for this lesson:

| | | | | |
|---|---|---|---|---|
| enforce | lava | peak | exert | interior |
| smart | gingerly | vanish | erupt | volcano |

>>>> *There are six blank spaces in the story below. Four vocabulary words have already been used in the story. They are underlined. Use the other six words to fill in the blanks.*

A <u>volcano</u> is active when the <u>interior</u> gases can push their way upward to the surface. An active volcano can produce rivers of molten _____lava_____.

A volcano is inactive if it cannot _____erupt_____.

One must _____exert_____ caution when visiting an active volcano. You must step <u>gingerly</u> around the crater. Careless people have been known to fall into the crater and suddenly _____vanish_____. To prevent such accidents, officials _____enforce_____ strict safety regulations.

While on the <u>peak</u> of an active volcano, a visitor might have to use a handkerchief to cover his or her mouth. The gases can burn your throat and make your eyes _____smart_____.

## Learn More About Volcanoes

>>>> *On a separate sheet of paper or in your notebook or journal, complete one or more of the activities below.*

### Building Language

Several of the vocabulary words in this selection can be confusing because they seem to have more than one meaning. Write definitions for *smart* and *peak*. Then look up and write another meaning for the words. Now write a definition for the word *gingerly*. How could this word be easily misunderstood?

### Working Together

Create a three-dimensional map of the world with the major volcanoes labeled. Divide up the tasks so that some people are researching volcanoes in different continents and others are constructing and labeling the map. Display your map in the classroom.

### Learning Across the Curriculum

The eruption of Mount Vesuvius in Pompeii, Italy, in A.D. 79 was remarkable for what was preserved when the lava poured over the unsuspecting town. Look up information about the destruction of Pompeii. Pretend you are a news reporter on the scene, broadcasting the news of what has happened. Write a radio report, explaining the eruption and its results.

The proud colt steps into the auction ring. He is turned in slow circles. His brown coat has been brushed to a high **gloss.** The horse breeders study the thoroughbred. The **auctioneer** begins his **chant.** The bidding starts at a quarter of a million dollars. Quickly, the price rises to a half a million. Breeders from many different countries **compete** against one another. The final bid is one and a half million dollars. The colt now has an owner.

The Keeneland race course in Kentucky is the scene of many multimillion-dollar bids. Buyers look for a horse with an excellent **pedigree.** In this way, they improve the bloodlines of their stables.

One likely colt sold for $4.5 million. He was the son of the great racehorse Nijinsky II. Even more amazing are the prices paid when groups of people buy horses **jointly.** In shared ownership, each partner has the right to breed the horse once a year. Conquistador Cielo was bought this way for over $36 million! His owners hoped he would **sire** many winners.

Splendid **banquets** are given to attract horse buyers to auctions. These banquets have become a **permanent** part of the auction scene. In addition to enjoying themselves, buyers study each horse carefully. Future owners **investigate** every aspect of a horse before bidding. They even use computers to trace bloodlines. Buying racehorses is no small matter. Going once, going twice. . . sold!

## UNDERSTANDING THE STORY

>>>> *Circle the letter next to each correct statement.*

1. The main idea of this story is that
   a. huge sums of money are spent at auctions on horses that can win races and sire other great racehorses.
   b. buying horses jointly helps breeders to afford them.
   c. the use of computers in tracing bloodlines has revolutionized the business of buying racehorses.

2. From this story, you can conclude that
   a. thoroughbreds will soon be inexpensive because there will be so many of them.
   b. the record price paid for Conquistador Cielo will not seem high in years to come.
   c. a flowing mane and large front hooves are signs of a great racehorse.

# MAKE AN ALPHABETICAL LIST

>>>> *Here are the ten vocabulary words in this lesson. Write them in alphabetical order in the spaces below.*

| gloss | permanent | auctioneer | jointly | compete |
| sire | investigate | banquets | chant | pedigree |

1. _____auctioneer_____
2. _____banquets_____
3. _____chant_____
4. _____compete_____
5. _____gloss_____

6. _____investigate_____
7. _____jointly_____
8. _____pedigree_____
9. _____permanent_____
10. _____sire_____

# WHAT DO THE WORDS MEAN?

>>>> *Following are some meanings, or definitions, for the ten vocabulary words in this lesson. Write the words next to their definitions.*

1. _____compete_____ to oppose; to try for the same thing

2. _____auctioneer_____ the agent in charge of selling at an auction

3. _____banquets_____ formal meals; lavish feasts

4. _____gloss_____ high polish; shine

5. _____investigate_____ to study; to look into carefully

6. _____jointly_____ together; in partnership

7. _____sire_____ to be the father of

8. _____chant_____ rapid and rhythmic speaking

9. _____pedigree_____ the record of an animal's ancestors, especially with respect to purity of breed

10. _____permanent_____ lasting; continuing

# COMPLETE THE SENTENCES

>>>> *Use the vocabulary words in this lesson to complete the following sentences. Use each word only once.*

| | | | | |
|---|---|---|---|---|
| chant | sire | auctioneer | jointly | permanent |
| banquets | gloss | compete | pedigree | investigate |

1. When the ___auctioneer___ banged her gavel on the stand, it meant that the sale was over.

2. The auctioneer's ___chant___ sounded like a tuneless song.

3. Great ___banquets___ are served at horse auctions in order to attract bidders.

4. The tension in the room rises as breeders ___compete___ against one another.

5. A breeder will ___investigate___ a horse's health and bloodline before bidding.

6. A breeder wants to be sure that the ___pedigree___ of a horse is a good one.

7. Buyers sometimes get together and purchase a horse ___jointly___.

8. A good diet and daily brushing give a high ___gloss___ to a horse's coat.

9. A horse can ___sire___ many young, but only a few may grow up to be great racehorses.

10. A racehorse often becomes a be ___permanent___ part of a well-known stable.

# USE YOUR OWN WORDS

>>>> *Look at the picture. What words come into your mind other than the ten vocabulary words used in this lesson? Write them on the lines below. To help you get started, here are two good words:*

1. ___bidder___
2. ___ropes___
3. ___Answers will vary.___
4. _____
5. _____
6. _____
7. _____
8. _____
9. _____
10. _____

# IDENTIFY THE SYNONYMS AND ANTONYMS

>>>> A **synonym** is a word that means the same, or nearly the same, as another word. An **antonym** is a word that means the opposite of another word.

>>>> *There are six vocabulary words listed below. To the right of each is either a synonym or an antonym. On the line beside each pair of words, write S for synonyms or A for antonyms.*

| | | | | |
|---|---|---|---|---|
| 1. | **compete** | cooperate | 1. | A |
| 2. | **pedigree** | history | 2. | S |
| 3. | **jointly** | separately | 3. | A |
| 4. | **banquets** | fancy meals | 4. | S |
| 5. | **permanent** | temporary | 5. | A |
| 6. | **auctioneer** | buyer | 6. | A |

# COMPLETE THE STORY

>>>> Here are the ten vocabulary words for this lesson:

| | | | | |
|---|---|---|---|---|
| compete | sire | auctioneer | banquets | pedigree |
| investigate | gloss | permanent | chant | jointly |

>>>> *There are six blank spaces in the story below. Four vocabulary words have already been used in the story. They are underlined. Use the other six words to fill in the blanks.*

Horse auctions are exciting. The horses' coats are brushed to a high _____gloss_____. The _____auctioneer_____ leads the show with a <u>chant</u> that is rapid and singsong. Tasty and attractive _____banquets_____ are served to bring in buyers. These feasts have become a _____permanent_____ part of the scene.

You can be sure that buyers _____investigate_____ every detail of a horse's history before bidding. The <u>pedigree</u> is studied to see how many of the horse's ancestors were winners. The breeders <u>compete</u> for horses with excellent records.

Because racehorses are so costly, people often decide to buy them _____jointly_____ . They hope that the horse will <u>sire</u> many great racers.

## Learn More About Racing Horses

>>>> *On a separate sheet of paper or in your notebook or journal, complete one or more of the activities below.*

### Learning Across the Curriculum

Owning horses and racing them are very costly. Research the expenses involved in owning, training, and racing a horse. Find out how much the average racehorse costs its owner a year. Give a presentation to your classmates.

### Broadening Your Understanding

The Kentucky Derby is one of the most celebrated horse races in the United States. Find out the history of this race and write about it. Include information about some of the most famous winners of the Kentucky Derby. Present your findings to the class.

### Extending Your Reading

Writer Dick Francis is a jockey who became a mystery writer. He never forgot his love of horses, and his books are all mysteries about horses. Listed below are several of his books. Read one. Then write a paragraph and discuss whether you think the information in his book about the business of horses is realistic.

*Blood Sport*
*Bolt*
*Bone Crack*
*Forfeit*
*Hot Money*

One of the most mysterious places in the world is Stonehenge, in England. Here, an ancient $\boxed{monument}$ of rock dominates the landscape.

At Stonehenge, there are three circles of huge stones, one inside the other. Each stone is $\boxed{approximately}$ 14 feet high and weighs about 28 tons. Next to each stone in the outer circle is a shallow pit. Inside the smallest circle are stones shaped like horseshoes. At the center is a fallen stone that could have been an altar.

The rocks of Stonehenge still $\boxed{perplex}$ scientists today. Carvings on the stones $\boxed{denote}$ that they were put there about 4,000 years ago. Some $\boxed{pundits}$ believe Stonehenge was built for sun worship. Others say it might have been built by $\boxed{pagan}$ priests as a temple or a $\boxed{burial}$ place. $\boxed{Cremated}$ bodies have been found in the pits. Still other people believe Stonehenge was an $\boxed{astronomical}$ calendar used to tell the seasons of the year and $\boxed{eclipses}$ of the sun and moon.

There are also many questions about how the stones got there. Were the stones hauled by hand or floated in on rafts? How were they raised to an upright position?

No one has been able to answer these questions. Stonehenge remains one of the world's biggest mysteries.

## UNDERSTANDING THE STORY

 *Circle the letter next to each correct statement.*

1. The main idea of this story is that
   a. most scientists believe Stonehenge was an astronomical calendar.
   (b.) the origin of Stonehenge remains a mystery, although many theories have been suggested.
   c. Stonehenge is considered one of the seven wonders of the world.

2. The fact that human ashes were found in the pits at Stonehenge suggests that
   a. the area was used as a battlefield.
   b. the stones are what is left of a larger structure that burned to the ground.
   (c.) bodies were often cremated before burial in ancient times.

# MAKE AN ALPHABETICAL LIST

>>>> *Here are the ten vocabulary words in this lesson. Write them in alphabetical order in the spaces below.*

| | | | | |
|---|---|---|---|---|
| monument | burial | perplex | approximately | denote |
| pundits | pagan | cremated | astronomical | eclipses |

1. approximately

2. astronomical

3. burial

4. cremated

5. denote

6. eclipses

7. monument

8. pagan

9. perplex

10. pundits

# WHAT DO THE WORDS MEAN?

>>>> *Following are some meanings, or definitions, for the ten vocabulary words in this lesson. Write the words next to their definitions.*

1. cremated — burned to ashes

2. pundits — persons who have knowledge of a subject

3. perplex — to puzzle; to confuse

4. denote — to show; to point out

5. eclipses — times when the sun or moon cannot be seen because its light is blocked

6. monument — something from a past age that is believed to have historical importance

7. astronomical — having to do with astronomy; the study of planets, stars, and other bodies in outer space

8. pagan — a follower of a religion with many gods

9. burial — having to do with placing a body in its final resting place

10. approximately — nearly; about

# COMPLETE THE SENTENCES

>>>> *Use the vocabulary words in this lesson to complete the following sentences. Use each word only once.*

| pundits | monument | denote | cremated | eclipses |
|---------|----------|--------|----------|----------|
| pagan | astronomical | perplex | burial | approximately |

1. A question that continues to _____perplex_____ scientists is what was the purpose of Stonehenge.

2. Stonehenge may have predicted _____eclipses_____ of the sun and moon.

3. In fact, drawings of ancient ___astronomical___ calendars show structures that look much like Stonehenge.

4. Priests of a _____pagan_____ religion may have meant the stones to be a temple.

5. Carvings on the stones _____denote_____ that Stonehenge is about 4,000 years old.

6. One of the things that _____pundits_____ wonder is what the purpose of the Stonehenge monument was.

7. The ashes of _____cremated_____ bodies were found in the area of the outer circle.

8. Stonehenge may have been a sacred _____burial_____ place.

9. A wall of earth __approximately__ 320 feet in diameter surrounds the stones.

10. The _____monument_____ of Stonehenge stands as a reminder of ancient people.

# USE YOUR OWN WORDS

>>>> *Look at the picture. What words come into your mind other than the ten vocabulary words used in this lesson? Write them on the lines below. To help you get started, here are two good words:*

1. _____grass_____
2. _____sky_____
3. ___Answers will vary.___
4. _____
5. _____
6. _____
7. _____
8. _____
9. _____
10. _____

>>>> In an **analogy,** similar relationships occur between words that are different. For example, *pig* is to *hog* as *car* is to *automobile.* The relationship is that the words mean the same. Here's another analogy: *noisy* is to *quiet* as *short* is to *tall.* In this relationship, the words have opposite meanings.

>>>> *See if you can complete the following analogies. Circle the correct word or words.*

1. **Denote** is to **point out** as **dominates** is to

   **a.** rises above   **b.** towers over   **c.** grows up   **d.** climbs over

2. **Stonehenge** is to **monument** as **eclipses** is to

   **a.** sunlight   **b.** planets   **c.** heavenly bodies   **d.** blackouts

3. **Mysterious** is to **strange** as **ancient** is to

   **a.** approximately   **b.** old   **c.** pagan   **d.** astronomical

4. **Perplex** is to **confuse** as **cremated** is to

   **a.** boiled   **b.** buried   **c.** cooled   **d.** burned

5. **Erected** is to **destroyed** as **upright** is to

   **a.** fallen   **b.** vertical   **c.** approximately   **d.** astronomical

# COMPLETE THE STORY

>>>> Here are the ten vocabulary words for this lesson:

| | | | | |
|---|---|---|---|---|
| monument | approximately | cremated | denote | pundits |
| pagan | perplex | astronomical | eclipses | burial |

>>>> *There are six blank spaces in the story below. Four vocabulary words have already been used in the story. They are underlined. Use the other six words to fill in the blanks.*

The rock _____monument_____ of Stonehenge dominated the Salisbury Plains in England.

The rocks of Stonehenge still _____perplex_____ pundits today. Some believe Stonehenge was an _____astronomical_____ calendar that predicted eclipses of the moon and sun. Others think it was used as a _____pagan_____ temple or _____burial_____ place. Cremated bodies have been found there. Carvings denote the stones were erected _____approximately_____ 4,000 years ago.

Despite modern science, Stonehenge remains a mystery.

## Learn More About Ancient Science

>>>> *On a separate sheet of paper or in your notebook or journal, complete one or more of the activities below.*

### Working Together

Scientists have many theories about why Stonehenge was built. Research the theories and assign one student to find out about each theory. Then have a debate with each person defending the theory he or she researched. Have the class vote to decide which person was most persuasive.

### Learning Across the Curriculum

The Mayans, the Egyptians, and many other ancient civilizations had ways of telling time. Research the way one of these peoples kept track of time and write a paragraph explaining it. If you can, build a model and demonstrate it for the class.

### Broadening Your Understanding

Find out more about the Druids, who scientists believe built Stonehenge. Write a description of what they believed and how they lived. Also write something about their history.

As a child, Georgia O'Keeffe showed a talent for art. She enjoyed expressing her feelings in images. One day Alfred Stieglitz, a famous critic and photographer, saw some of her work. He liked it so much that he ⟨*exhibited*⟩ her paintings in a one-woman show. That show, in 1916, made O'Keeffe's reputation as an important artist. She married Stieglitz. He encouraged her to express her vision in her own way. Giant flowers, barns, sharply drawn buildings, and bright landscapes emerged from her brush.

O'Keeffe's paintings display freshness and ⟨*vigor.*⟩ Her works vary a great deal. This makes ⟨*classification*⟩ of her style difficult. Some critics label her a ⟨*romanticist.*⟩ Others say she is a realist.

O'Keeffe moved to New Mexico. ⟨*Rural,*⟩ or country, scenes appealed to her. She found them ⟨*preferable*⟩ to urban, or city, subjects. Canyons, adobe houses, and ⟨*vast*⟩ landscapes of the Southwest appeared in many of her paintings. She painted a skull ⟨*ornamented*⟩ with a bright flower to show life and death together. Some of her paintings became dreamy and ⟨*impressionistic.*⟩ Others were sharp and clear.

Georgia O'Keeffe died in 1986. Her popularity continues to increase. In 1989, an O'Keeffe ⟨*retrospective*⟩ was exhibited in major museums across the country, an honor reserved for the best artists.

## UNDERSTANDING THE STORY

>>>> *Circle the letter next to each correct statement.*

1. The main idea of this story is that
   a. Georgia O'Keeffe was married to famous critic and photographer Alfred Stieglitz.
   b. the variety and vigor of O'Keeffe's painting place her among the best artists of this century.
   c. O'Keeffe's paintings usually show rural rather than urban scenes.

2. From this story, you can conclude that
   a. the American Academy of Arts and Letters elected O'Keeffe a member on the basis of her skull paintings alone.
   b. O'Keeffe's career as a painter ended when she married Stieglitz.
   c. O'Keeffe's paintings present her personal vision of life in a way that appeals to many people.

# MAKE AN ALPHABETICAL LIST

>>>> *Here are the ten vocabulary words in this lesson. Write them in alphabetical order in the spaces below.*

| | | | | |
|---|---|---|---|---|
| retrospective | romanticist | exhibited | vast | classification |
| ornamented | rural | preferable | vigor | impressionistic |

1. classification
2. exhibited
3. impressionistic
4. ornamented
5. preferable

6. retrospective
7. romanticist
8. rural
9. vast
10. vigor

# WHAT DO THE WORDS MEAN?

>>>> *Following are some meanings, or definitions, for the ten vocabulary words in this lesson. Write the words next to their definitions.*

1. classification — putting something into a special group or class

2. exhibited — displayed; shown to the public

3. preferable — something liked better; more desirable

4. vast — huge; spacious

5. vigor — strength; vitality

6. retrospective — an exhibition of the life work of an artist

7. rural — having to do with open country and farming

8. ornamented — decorated; made more beautiful

9. romanticist — one who paints people and things as she or he would like them to be rather than as they really are

10. impressionistic — in the style of painting in which the painter tries to catch a momentary glimpse of the subject

>>>> *Use the vocabulary words in this lesson to complete the following sentences. Use each word only once.*

| vigor | vast | preferable | classification | impressionistic |
| romanticist | rural | ornamented | retrospective | exhibited |

1. __Impressionistic__ painters try to capture the effect of sunlight in their paintings.

2. __Classification__ of O'Keeffe's work is difficult because different styles appear in it.

3. A __romanticist__ is likely to paint landscapes.

4. O'Keeffe was a young, unknown artist when Stieglitz __exhibited__ her work.

5. The brush strokes in O'Keeffe's paintings show __vigor__ and spirit.

6. The __vast__ lands of New Mexico greatly impressed O'Keeffe.

7. Though most of her paintings are simple, some are __ornamented__ with brightly colored leaves and flowers.

8. As a child, O'Keeffe found it __preferable__ to express herself in painted images.

9. After her death, many museums displayed the O'Keeffe __retrospective__.

10. Houses made of adobe are common in the __rural__ Southwest.

## USE YOUR OWN WORDS

>>>> *Look at the picture. What words come into your mind other than the ten vocabulary words used in this lesson? Write them on the lines below. To help you get started, here are two good words:*

1. _____work_____
2. _____shapes_____
3. ___Answers will vary.___
4. _____
5. _____
6. _____
7. _____
8. _____
9. _____
10. _____

# FIND SOME SYNONYMS

>>>> A **synonym** is a word that means the same, or nearly the same, as another word. *Sorrowful* and *sad* are synonyms.

>>>> *The story you read has many interesting words that were not highlighted as vocabulary words. Six of these words are* **vary, scene, critic, express, talent,** *and* **vision.** *Can you think of a synonym for each of these words? Write the synonym in the blank space next to the word.*

**1.** vary      differ; change

**2.** scene      setting; location

**3.** critic      judge; reviewer

**4.** express      say; reveal

**5.** talent      skill; ability

**6.** vision      imagination; thoughts

# COMPLETE THE STORY

>>>> Here are the ten vocabulary words for this lesson:

| | | | | |
|---|---|---|---|---|
| retrospective | vigor | classification | impressionistic | preferable |
| romanticist | vast | ornamented | rural | exhibited |

>>>> *There are six blank spaces in the story below. Four vocabulary words have already been used in the story. They are underlined. Use the other six words to fill in the blanks.*

When Alfred Stieglitz first _____exhibited_____ the works of Georgia O'Keeffe, the critics were amazed. They found it hard to believe that this artist painted so well in so many styles. <u>Classification</u> of her paintings into one group seemed impossible. Some viewers thought her art was _____impressionistic_____ in style. Others said that she was a <u>romanticist</u> in her outlook. She soon achieved a reputation as one of the finest artists in the United States.

O'Keeffe's paintings show a <u>vigor</u> that is inspiring. The dried bones and _____vast_____ deserts she paints are often brightly _____ornamented_____ with huge flowers or plants. While urban artists find it <u>preferable</u> to paint city scenes, her works show scenes of _____rural_____ life. People could see examples of her different styles in the _____retrospective_____ displayed after her death.

**108**

## Learn More About Artists

>>>> *On a separate sheet of paper or in your notebook or journal, complete one or more of the activities below.*

### Appreciating Diversity

Research the work of an artist who painted pictures of the landscape in a region or country in which you are interested. Also look at photographs of this area. How did the artist interpret the landscape?

### Learning Across the Curriculum

Georgia O'Keeffe is not the only artist to be inspired by the American Southwest. Find an example of the work of painter R.C. Gorman or another Native American artist. Write a paragraph describing how you think the Southwest landscape is reflected in the work.

### Broadening Your Understanding

Find a book with photographs of Georgia O'Keeffe's paintings. Then imagine you have to describe them to people who cannot see. Write a description of the work that will help people who are blind understand O'Keeffe's work and its power.

# 19 THE TOWER OF PARIS

When one thinks of famous **structures** of the world, the Eiffel Tower comes to mind. This **breathtaking** **landmark** rises 984 feet above Paris. It offers a grand **panorama** of the city.

A visitor can take an elevator to any of the tower's three observation floors. From each **platform,** the camera bug can take pictures of the city. These photos will surely become treasured **souvenirs.** The visitor gets a splendid view of the Cathedral of Notre Dame, the Seine River, and the Louvre, one of the world's leading art museums. **Binoculars** are available for closeup viewing of these great sights.

The tower was designed by the man for whom it was named—Alexandre-Gustave Eiffel. It was built for an **exposition** in 1889. Nothing like it had ever been built before. It was constructed in less than a year at small cost. The Eiffel Tower remained the tallest building in the world for 41 years. (The Chrysler Building in New York topped it in 1930.)

There is a restaurant on the first floor of the tower. Here, the visitor can hear **expressions** of wonder in many languages. Tourists from all over the world make a point of visiting the tower.

For the tourist from any nation, the memories of visiting the Eiffel Tower will **endure** forever.

## UNDERSTANDING THE STORY

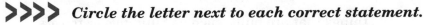 *Circle the letter next to each correct statement.*

1. The main purpose of this story is to
   a. list the many historical landmarks in Paris.
   (b.) describe probably the most famous landmark in Paris.
   c. tell of the struggles that Alexandre-Gustave Eiffel had in building the tower.

2. From this story, you can conclude that
   a. the Eiffel Tower is taller than the World Trade Center in New York City.
   b. Paris is the most popular city in Europe.
   (c.) the loss of the Eiffel Tower would be a serious blow to French tourism.

# MAKE AN ALPHABETICAL LIST

>>>> *Here are the ten vocabulary words in this lesson. Write them in alphabetical order in the spaces below.*

| | | | | |
|---|---|---|---|---|
| exposition | platform | landmark | panorama | souvenirs |
| expressions | breathtaking | structures | endure | binoculars |

1. binoculars
2. breathtaking
3. endure
4. exposition
5. expressions

6. landmark
7. panorama
8. platform
9. souvenirs
10. structures

# WHAT DO THE WORDS MEAN?

>>>> *Following are some meanings, or definitions, for the ten vocabulary words in this lesson. Write the words next to their definitions.*

1. panorama — a wide view of a surrounding region
2. breathtaking — very exciting; thrilling
3. expressions — sounds or actions that show some feelings
4. platform — a raised level surface
5. structures — things that are built, such as buildings or towers
6. landmark — something familiar or easily seen
7. binoculars — glasses used to magnify faraway objects
8. exposition — public show or exhibition
9. souvenirs — things bought or kept for remembrance
10. endure — to last; to keep on

# COMPLETE THE SENTENCES

>>>> *Use the vocabulary words in this lesson to complete the following sentences. Use each word only once.*

| souvenirs | binoculars | expressions | structures | platform |
|-----------|-----------|-------------|------------|----------|
| breathtaking | exposition | panorama | endure | landmark |

1. At an ___exposition___, products of science, industry, and art are displayed.

2. Among the well-known ___structures___ in Paris, the Eiffel Tower is the most famous.

3. Just as the Washington Monument is a national ___landmark___ in the United States, the Eiffel Tower is one in France.

4. The view from the observation deck is ___breathtaking___.

5. This deck serves as an ideal ___platform___ from which to take pictures.

6. Tourists return with ___souvenirs___ from their tour of Europe.

7. Many tourists carry ___binoculars___ with them so they can get close-up views.

8. You can hear ___expressions___ as visitors look at the view.

9. For a ___panorama___ of New York City, go to the top of the World Trade Center.

10. To help the Eiffel Tower ___endure___ for years to come, it is well cared for.

# USE YOUR OWN WORDS

>>>> *Look at the picture. What words come into your mind other than the ten vocabulary words used in this lesson? Write them on the lines below. To help you get started, here are two good words:*

1. ___graceful___
2. ___tall___
3. ___Answers will vary.___
4. _____
5. _____
6. _____
7. _____
8. _____
9. _____
10. _____

# DESCRIBE THE NOUNS

>>>> *The two vocabulary words below are nouns. List as many words as you can that describe or tell something about the words* panorama *and* structure. *You can work on this with your classmates.*

Answers may vary.

### panorama
1. _____ wide _____
2. _____ pretty _____
3. _____ colorful _____
4. _____ unusual _____
5. _____ view _____
6. _____ scenic _____
7. _____ vast _____
8. _____ beautiful _____

### structure
1. _____ tall _____
2. _____ sturdy _____
3. _____ elegant _____
4. _____ lasting _____
5. _____ magnificent _____
6. _____ crumbling _____
7. _____ historic _____
8. _____ stately _____

# COMPLETE THE STORY

>>>> Here are the ten vocabulary words for this lesson:

| breathtaking | landmark | souvenirs | panorama | exposition |
|---|---|---|---|---|
| platform | expressions | binoculars | endure | structures |

>>>> *There are six blank spaces in the story below. Four vocabulary words have already been used in the story. They are underlined. Use the other six words to fill in the blanks.*

When the Eiffel Tower was built for an ____exposition____ back in 1889, it was the tallest of all <u>structures</u> in Paris. Today this ____landmark____ is still one of the wonders of the world.

Many ____expressions____ of wonder have been used to describe the Eiffel Tower's view. Indeed, the observation deck offers a <u>breathtaking</u> ____panorama____ of the city. A visitor can take a close look by using ____binoculars____.

Tourists may take advantage of a restaurant on the bottom <u>platform</u> and a stand where they may purchase ____souvenirs____.

The Eiffel Tower will continue to <u>endure</u> as one of the world's premier attractions.

## Learn More About Architecture

**>>>>** *On a separate sheet of paper or in your notebook or journal, complete one or more of the activities below.*

### Working Together

Design a city of the future with your classmates. Divide up responsibilities so that different people are responsible for different parts of the city design. Parts of the city that need to be designed include streets, office buildings, stores, homes, recreational buildings, schools, hospitals, and public buildings, such as libraries and government offices. When everyone has designed his or her part of the city, draw a map. The map should show the city's buildings as if someone were looking down on the city from an airplane. You may also want to include drawings that show what the city will look like at street level.

### Learning Across the Curriculum

Today skyscrapers are constructed in ways that the designer of the Eiffel Tower wouldn't have dreamed of. Find out some details about how skyscrapers are made today and write a brief explanation of what goes into the construction. If you wish, make a diagram of the inside of a skyscraper and explain some of the elements of its design.

### Broadening Your Understanding

Check out a guidebook of Paris. Read about the architecture of the city. Then write a description of the five buildings you would most like to see in Paris and why. Explain something about the history of each building.

On a *humid* summer night in 1986, Midori Goto prepared to take a bow. The 14-year-old violinist was *stunned* by what happened next. The audience cheered and whistled wildly. Then the *conductor* and musicians of the Boston Symphony *Orchestra* hugged and kissed her.

The young concert violinist had just played Leonard Bernstein's *Serenade*. Her performance was "technically near-perfect." But that was only part of the story. Near the end of this long, *elaborate* piece, one of the strings on her violin snapped. Without missing a beat, she borrowed the concertmaster's violin and continued. Then, unbelievably, another string broke. Again she switched violins and continued playing. The new violins were larger than the one this *diminutive* girl was used to. But Midori finished the concert. She later explained, "I didn't want to stop. I love that piece."

Japanese-born Midori Goto was a child *prodigy.* At age 10, Goto was accepted by the *renowned* Juilliard School in New York City. She went on to play with some of the world's best-known violinists.

But on that magical night in 1986, Goto's whole life changed. She became famous. Yet Goto remained an *unaffected* teenager. While on tour, she still liked to *frolic* with her Snoopy doll.

Now in her twenties, Goto gives free concerts for children in the United States and Japan. She wants to share her love of music with them and get them as excited as she is about music from the great composers. Sometimes, she even gives free violin lessons!

## UNDERSTANDING THE STORY

>>>> *Circle the letter next to each correct statement.*

1. The main idea of this story is that
   a. Midori Goto switched violins twice during a performance.
   b. Goto has performed with some of the best-known violinists in the world.
   c. Goto has proved to be a talented violinist and a determined young lady who enjoys life.

2. From this story, you can conclude that
   a. Midori Goto will not give up easily.
   b. Goto will continue to break violin strings during her concerts.
   c. Goto will return to the Juilliard School.

**117**

# MAKE AN ALPHABETICAL LIST

>>>> *Here are the ten vocabulary words in this lesson. Write them in alphabetical order in the spaces below.*

| elaborate | frolic | orchestra | unaffected | diminutive |
| conductor | stunned | prodigy | humid | renowned |

1. _____ conductor _____   6. _____ orchestra _____
2. _____ diminutive _____   7. _____ prodigy _____
3. _____ elaborate _____   8. _____ renowned _____
4. _____ frolic _____   9. _____ stunned _____
5. _____ humid _____   10. _____ unaffected _____

# WHAT DO THE WORDS MEAN?

>>>> *Following are some meanings, or definitions, for the ten vocabulary words in this lesson. Write the words next to their definitions.*

1. _____ conductor _____ the leader of a group of musicians

2. _____ diminutive _____ very small; tiny

3. _____ unaffected _____ not influenced or changed; natural

4. _____ orchestra _____ musicians who perform together, especially for playing symphonies

5. _____ renowned _____ having a great reputation; famous

6. _____ elaborate _____ complicated; intricate

7. _____ humid _____ damp, moist air

8. _____ prodigy _____ a highly gifted or talented person, usually a child

9. _____ stunned _____ made senseless, dizzy; confused

10. _____ frolic _____ to play about happily

118

>>>> *Use the vocabulary words in this lesson to complete the following sentences. Use each word only once.*

| | | | | |
|---|---|---|---|---|
| elaborate | unaffected | renowned | frolic | prodigy |
| humid | stunned | diminutive | orchestra | conductor |

1. We don't expect to see famous musicians _____frolic_____ with a doll.

2. It is difficult to perform on a hot, _____humid_____ night.

3. Teachers at the Juilliard School knew Goto was a _____prodigy_____.

4. Goto was _____stunned_____ when the other musicians hugged and kissed her.

5. Goto, like all other musicians, had to follow the lead of the _____conductor_____.

6. Her performance at Tanglewood proved that Goto deserved to be _____renowned_____.

7. Goto looked especially _____diminutive_____ next to the taller musicians.

8. A musician must practice often to play an _____elaborate_____ piece like *Serenade*.

9. Goto's friends are glad that, in spite of her fame, she is still _____unaffected_____.

10. Members of the _____orchestra_____ were proud to be part of Goto's special night.

# USE YOUR OWN WORDS

>>>> *Look at the picture. What words come into your mind other than the ten vocabulary words used in this lesson? Write them on the lines below. To help you get started, here are two good words:*

1. _____performer_____

2. _____violin_____

3. _____Answers will vary._____

4. _____

5. _____

6. _____

7. _____

8. _____

9. _____

10. _____

# MAKE NEW WORDS FROM OLD

>>>> *Look at the vocabulary word orchestra. See how many words you can form by using the letters of this word. Write at least ten words in the spaces below.*

Answers may vary.

## orchestra

1. _____ or _____
2. _____ rest _____
3. _____ chest _____
4. _____ chore _____
5. _____ chat _____
6. _____ coarse _____
7. _____ horse _____
8. _____ hoarse _____
9. _____ set _____
10. _____ sort _____

# COMPLETE THE STORY

>>>> Here are the ten vocabulary words for this lesson:

| elaborate | unaffected | orchestra | frolic | renowned |
|-----------|-----------|-----------|--------|----------|
| humid | conductor | diminutive | stunned | prodigy |

>>>> *There are six blank spaces in the story below. Four vocabulary words have already been used in the story. They are underlined. Use the other six words to fill in the blanks.*

Goto's parents knew their child was a <u>prodigy</u>. Yet even they must have been _____ stunned _____ by her performance at Tanglewood. The <u>conductor</u> hugged and kissed her. So did the musicians in the _____ orchestra _____. They all realized that the hot, _____ humid _____ weather had made it hard to perform. They also realized that the music was long and _____ elaborate _____. How difficult this experience must have been for the <u>diminutive</u> girl! Goto surely deserves to be _____ renowned _____. But she never felt too important to _____ frolic _____ like a child. Who could have expected her to remain so <u>unaffected</u> after all that attention?

## Learn More About Musicians

>>>> *On a separate sheet of paper or in your notebook or journal, complete one or more of the activities below.*

### Appreciating Diversity

Research your favorite musician. Find out what you can about the musician and write a report about him or her. What has helped the person succeed? What kind of music does he or she play?

### Learning Across the Curriculum

The many kinds of instruments in an orchestra make music in different ways. Choose an instrument in which you are interested and find out the science behind the music. Write a description of how the instrument you chose makes music. You may want to make an illustration to help explain what you learn.

### Broadening Your Understanding

Go to the library and check out one of Midori Goto recordings. Several of her recordings are listed below. Listen to her perform. Then write a review of what you hear. What parts did you like? Would you recommend a classical concert to your friends? If you cannot find one of Goto's recordings, listen to a recording by another violinist.

Bartok, *Violin Concertos 1 and 2*
Paganini, Niccolo, *24 caprices, op. 1*
*Live at Carnegie Hall*

# Glossary

## A

**abrupt** *[uh BRUHPT]* sudden

**activist** *[AK tiv ist]* a person who publicly supports a cause

**actual** *[AHK chu uhl]* real

**affiliate** *[af FIL ee it]* a person or an organization usually connected to a larger organization

**altered** *[AWL turd]* changed

**anguish** *[AYNG gwihsh]* pain; sorrow

**apology** *[uh PAWL uh jee]* an expression of regret for wrongdoing

**apparatus** *[ap uh RAT us]* materials, tools, special instruments, or machinery needed to carry out a purpose

**apparel** *[uh PAIR ul]* clothing; dress

**apply** *[uh PLY]* to seek a job; to ask for work

**appropriate** *[uh PRO pree it]* proper

**approximately** *[uh PROK suh mit lee]* nearly; about

**aptitude** *[AP tih tood]* a natural ability or capacity; a talent

**arrested** *[uh REST ed]* held by the police

**assignments** *[uh SYN mihnts]* definite tasks or jobs to be done; specific works to be accomplished

**astronomical** *[as truh NOM uh kul]* having to do with astronomy; the study of planets, stars, and other bodies in outer space

**attained** *[uh TAYND]* reached; achieved

**auctioneer** *[AWK shun eer]* the agent in charge of selling at an auction

**authorities** *[uh THOR ih teez]* specialists

**await** *[uh WAYT]* to wait for; to expect

## B

**banished** *[BAN isht]* forced to leave one's country

**banquets** *[BAN kwits]* formal meals; lavish feasts

**barriers** *[BAIR ee uhrz]* obstacles; walls

**binoculars** *[buh NOK yuh lurz]* glasses used to magnify faraway objects

**blessed** *[BLES id]* given great happiness

**bolted** *[BOHL tid]* fastened; held with metal fittings

**breathtaking** *[BRETH tayk ing]* very exciting; thrilling

**burial** *[BEHR ee uhl]* having to do with placing a body in its final resting place

## C

**carnage** *[KAHR nij]* the killing of a great number of people or animals

**cello** *[CHEL oh]* a musical instrument similar to a violin, but much larger, that is played in a sitting position

**challenge** *[CHAL unj]* a call to a contest or battle

**chant** *[CHANT]* rapid and rhythmic speaking

**chasms** *[KAZ umz]* deep openings or cracks

**circumstances** *[SER kuhm stans ehz]* conditions

**clamor** *[KLAM ur]* to demand noisily; to call for loudly

## Classification (second column)

**classification** *[klas ih fih KAY shun]* putting something into a special group or class

**commend** *[kuh MEND]* to praise; to acclaim as worthy of notice

**compete** *[kom PEET]* to oppose; to try for the same thing

**conductor** *[kuhn DUK tuhr]* the leader of a group of musicians

**conservationists** *[kon sur VAY shu nists]* persons who wish to save forms of animals and plant life in danger of being destroyed forever

**considerable** *[kun SID ur uh bul]* not a little; much

**contract** *[KON trakt]* a legal paper promising a job

**cradle** *[KRAY dul]* a framework upon which a ship rests, usually during repair

**cremated** *[KREE mayt id]* burned to ashes

**crescent** *[KRES unt]* the shape of the moon in the first or last quarter; the symbol of the Muslim religion

**cultural** *[KAHL chur uhl]* relating to the beliefs and behaviors of a social, ethnic, or religious group

## D

**dealt** *[DELT]* handled; managed; faced

**debut** *[DAY byoo]* a first appearance before the public

**define** *[duh FEYEN]* to explain the meaning of

**definitely** *[DEF ih nit lee]* absolutely

**denote** *[dih NOHT]* to show; to point out

**despite** *[dih SPEYET]* not prevented by; in spite of

**devoted** *[dee VOH tid]* gave up one's time, money, or efforts for some cause or person

**dictatorship** *[dik TAY tur ship]* the rule by one person or group that must be obeyed; power held by a few through force

**diminutive** *[dih MIN yoo tiv]* very small; tiny

**disciplinarian** *[dis uh plih NEHR ee uhn]* a person who believes in strict training

**documentary** *[dok yuh MEN tuh ree]* a factual presentation of a scene, place, or condition of life in writing or on film

**dwindled** *[DWIN duld]* reduced in number

**dynamic** *[deye NAM ihk]* full of energy; vigorous

## E

**eclipses** *[ee KLIP siz]* times when the sun or moon cannot be seen because its light is blocked

**efforts** *[EF furts]* attempts

**elaborate** *[ih LAB or uht]* complicated; intricate

**embodies** *[em BOD eez]* represents in real or definite form

**endure** *[en DYOOR]* to last; to keep on

**enforce** *[en FORS]* to make someone do something; to compel

**enthusiastic** *[en THOO zee AS tik]* eagerly interested

**erupt** *[ee RUPT]* to explode; to burst forth

**essential** *[ee SEN chul]* absolutely necessary

**exert** *[eg ZURT]* to apply; to use fully

**exhibited** *[eks ZIH bih tid]* displayed; shown to the public

**expedition** *[ek spuh DISH un]* group of people undertaking a special journey, such as mountain climbing

**explanation** *[ek spluh NAY shun]* a statement that clears up a difficulty or a mistake

**exposition** *[ek spoh ZISH un]* public show or exhibition

**expressions** *[ek SPRESH unz]* sounds or actions that show some feelings

**extermination** *[ek STUR mih NAY shun]* the act of destroying completely; putting an end to

## F

**falter** *[FAWL tuhr]* to hesitate; to fail or weaken

**fan** *[FAN]* an enthusiastic supporter

**fare** *[FAIR]* the cost of a ticket

**fascinated** *[FAS ih nay tid]* amazed; very interested by

**festivals** *[FES tih vulz]* celebrations

**fiction** *[FIK shun]* a story that is not true

**flawless** *[FLAW les]* perfect; without fault

**flirted** *[FLER tihd]* showed an interest

**forbears** *[FOR behrz]* family members who lived a long time ago

**frantic** *[FRAN tik]* wild with excitement; out of control

**frolic** *[FRO lik]* to play about happily

## G

**gingerly** *[JIN jur lee]* very carefully

**gloss** *[GLOS]* high polish; shine

**grave** *[GRAYV]* serious; critical

**grudge** *[GRUHJ]* resentment; ill feelings

## H

**hardy** *[HAHR dee]* able to take hard physical treatment; bold; daring

**harpoon** *[hahr POON]* a long spear with a rope tied to it used in killing a whale

**hoax** *[HOKS]* a trick

**humid** *[HYOO mid]* damp, moist air

## I

**identify** *[eye DEN tuh fy]* to recognize as being a particular person or thing

**ignorance** *[IG nur uns]* a lack of knowledge

**impressionistic** *[im preh shun IS tik]* in the style of painting in which the painter tries to catch a momentary glimpse of the subject

**informally** *[ihn FOOR mal lee]* a way of doing something that does not follow exact rules or procedures; casually

**instructors** *[ihn STRUHK tuhrs]* teachers; leaders

**intensive** *[ihn TENS ihv]* concentrated

**interior** *[in TEER ee ur]* inside; inner part

**investigate** *[in VES tih gayt]* to study; to look into carefully

**issues** *[ISH yooz]* topics or problems under discussion

## J

**jointly** *[JOINT lee]* together; in partnership

## L

**laden** *[LAY din]* loaded; heavily burdened

**landmark** *[LAND mark]* something familiar or easily seen

**lava** *[LAH vuh]* melted rock that comes from a volcano

**literacy** *[LIT ur uh see]* the ability to read and write

## M

**mammals** *[MAM ulz]* animals that feed milk to their young; people belong to this group

**manager** *[MAN ij ur]* a performer's business arranger

**margin** *[MAHR juhn]* a border; the space allowed for something

**matter** *[MAT ur]* a real thing; content rather than manner or style

**mere** *[MIR]* only; barely

**mingle** *[MING gul]* to mix; to get along together

**misery** *[MIZ uhr ee]* suffering; distress

**mission** *[MIH shun]* a special task

**monarch** *[MON ahrk]* a king or queen; an absolute ruler

**monument** *[MON yuh mehnt]* something from a past age that is believed to have historical importance

**motivated** *[MOH tuh vayt id]* stimulated to do something; inspired

## N

**notable** *[NOH tuh bul]* worthy of notice; remarkable

**novels** *[NAWV uhlz]* long stories about imaginary people and events

## O

**obligations** *[awb luh GAY shuns]* duties; responsibilities

**orchestra** *[OR kes truh]* musicians who perform together, especially for playing symphonies

**ornamented** *[OR nuh men tid]* decorated; made more beautiful

**ovations** *[oh VAY shunz]* bursts of loud clapping or cheering; waves of applause

## P

**pagan** *[PAY gun]* a follower of a religion with many gods

**panorama** *[pan uh RAM uh]* a wide view of a surrounding region

**peak** *[PEEK]* the top; the highest point

**pedigree** *[PED ih gree]* the record of an animal's ancestors, especially with respect to purity of breed

**perilous** *[PEHR uh lus]* dangerous; hazardous

**perished** *[PEHR isht]* died, usually in a violent manner

**permanent** *[PUR muh nehnt]* lasting; continuing

**perplex** *[pur PLEKS]* to puzzle; to confuse

**persisted** *[puhr SIHST uhd]* continued in spite of obstacles

**plastic** *[PLAS tik]* a synthetic or processed material

**platform** *[PLAT form]* a raised level surface

**plight** *[PLYT]* a condition or state, usually bad

**predicted** *[pree DIHKT uhd]* described what would happen in the future; forecasted

**preferable** *[PREH fir uh bul]* something liked better; more desirable

**prejudice** *[PREJ uh dihs]* dislike of people who are different

**primitive** *[PRIM uh tiv]* living long ago; from earliest times

**probable** *[PRAWB uh buhl]* likely to happen

**prodigy** *[PROD uh jee]* a highly gifted or talented person, usually a child

**products** *[PROD ukts]* manufactured items

**profession** *[pruh FESH un]* an occupation requiring an education

**project** *[PRAH jekt]* an undertaking, often a big, complicated job

**proof** *[PROOF]* facts; evidence

**prosperous** *[PROS per us]* successful

**protest** *[PROH test]* strong objection; opposition

**publication** *[pub le KAY shun]* the production of written material into printed form

**pundits** *[PUN ditz]* persons who have knowledge of a subject

**pursuing** *[pur SOO ing]* striving for

R

**racial** *[RAY shul]* of or having to do with race or origins

**recognition** *[rek ugh NIHSH uhn]* special notice or attention

**recognized** *[REK uhg NYZD]* identified

**reflect** *[ree FLEKT]* to give back an image of

**religious** *[ree LIJ us]* having to do with a belief in God; devout

**renditions** *[ren DISH uns]* performances or interpretations

**renowned** *[rih NOWND]* having a great reputation; famous

**reputable** *[REP yuh tuh bul]* honorable; well thought of

**resembles** *[ree ZEM bulz]* looks like; is similar in appearance

**restless** *[REHST luhs]* uneasy; bored

**restored** *[rih STORD]* brought back to its original state; reconstructed

**restricted** *[ree STRIKT id]* limited in freedom or use

**retrospective** *[RET roh SPEK TIV]* an exhibition of the life work of an artist

**romanticist** *[roh MAN tih sist]* one who paints people and things as she or he would like them to be rather than as they really are

**rural** *[RUR ul]* having to do with open country and farming

S

**sacred** *[SAY krid]* holy; worthy of reverence

**salvage** *[SAL vij]* the act of saving a ship or its cargo from the sea

**scale** *[SKAYL]* to climb

**scholarship** *[SKOL ur ship]* money given to help a student pay for studies

**segregation** *[seg ruh GAY shun]* separation from others; setting individuals or groups apart from society

**sheer** *[SHEER]* steep; straight up and down

**shrines** *[SHRYNZ]* sacred places; places where holy things are kept

**shy** *[SHY]* modest; uncertain

**sire** *[SEYER]* to be the father of

**skeptical** *[SKEP tuh kul]* having doubts; not willing to believe

**skillful** *[SKIL ful]* having ability gained by practice or knowledge; expert

**smart** *[SMAHRT]* to feel a sharp pain; to sting

**soared** *[SOHRD]* rose upward quickly

**souvenirs** *[SOO vuh NEERZ]* things bought or kept for remembrance

**spectacular** *[spek TAK yuh lur]* eye catching; very unusual

**structures** *[STRUK churz]* things that are built, such as buildings or towers

**stunned** *[STUND]* made senseless, dizzy; confused

**sullen** *[SUL uhn]* gloomy; resentful

**summit** *[SUM it]* the peak; the highest point

**symbols** *[SIM bulz]* things that stand for or represent something else; signs

**synonymous** *[si NON uh mus]* alike in meaning or significance

T

**talent** *[TAL unt]* a natural gift for doing something

**trade** *[TRAYD]* a job; a skill

**tremendous** *[tru MEN dus]* huge; enormous

**tyranny** *[TIR uh nee]* the cruel use of power

U

**unaffected** *[UN uh FEK tid]* not influenced or changed; natural

**urged** *[URJD]* advised strongly

V

**vanish** *[VAN ish]* to disappear

**vast** *[VAST]* huge; spacious

**vigor** *[VIHG uhr]* strength; vitality

**volcano** *[vol KAY noh]* a mountain with a cuplike crater that throws out hot melted rock and steam

**vulnerable** *[VUL nur uh bul]* defenseless against; open to attack or injury

W

**welfare** *[WEL fair]* happiness; well being